David Adam was born in A
Vicar of Danby on the No.
years, where he discovered the gift for writing prayers in the
Celtic pattern. His first book of these, *The Edge of Glory*,
achieved immediate popularity. He has since published sev-
eral collections of prayers and meditations based on the
Celtic tradition and the lives of the Celtic saints. His books
have been translated into various languages, including Finnish
and German, and have appeared in American editions. Many
of his prayers have now been set to music. After 13 years as
Vicar of Holy Island, where he had taken many retreats and
regularly taught school groups on prayer, David moved to
Waren Mill in Northumberland, from where he continues
his work and writing.

THE AWESOME JOURNEY

Life's pilgrimage

David Adam

First published in Great Britain in 2015

Society for Promoting Christian Knowledge
36 Causton Street
London SW1P 4ST
www.spck.org.uk

British Library Cataloguing-in-Publication Data
A catalogue record for this book is available from the British Library

ISBN 978–0–281–07294–1
eBook ISBN 978–0–281–07295–8

Typeset by Graphicraft Limited, Hong Kong
First printed in Great Britain by Ashford Colour Press
Subsequently digitally printed in Great Britain

eBook by Graphicraft Limited, Hong Kong

Produced on paper from sustainable forests

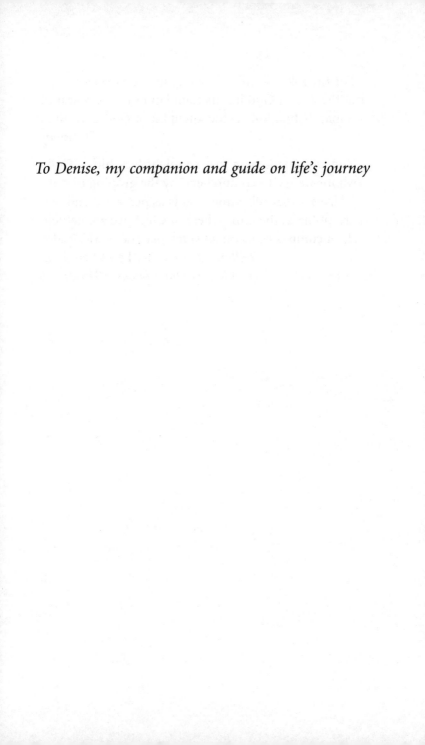

To Denise, my companion and guide on life's journey

For the sake of Greek learning men go overseas . . .
but the city of God has its foundation in every seat of
human habitation . . . the kingdom of God is within.
St Antony

God who made man that he might seek him – God
whom we try to comprehend by the groping of our
lives – that self-same God is as pervasive and
perceptible as the atmosphere in which we are bathed.
He encompasses us on all sides, like the world itself.
Teilhard de Chardin, Le Milieu divin
(London: Fontana Books, 1975), p. 46

❦ *Contents* ❦

✍ *Acknowledgements* ✍

I would like to thank SPCK for its continuing support and encouragement in my writing. I am especially grateful to Alison Barr for her friendship and guidance. I am indebted to many people who have shared this awesome journey with me, especially to Jackie Burn who taught me to 'Rejoice in the Lord' and to Denise who has been my constant companion as we journey on.

✒ Introduction ✒

For pilgrimage to be real it has to be a moving experience in more than simply a physical sense. True pilgrimage is about the opening of our eyes, our ears and our hearts, not simply about travelling. It has to do with relationships rather than with destinations; it involves seeing this world as God's world, and the people in it – including ourselves – as people loved by God. Pilgrimage is more about the heart than the soles of the feet! Too often Christians have given the impression that you should turn your back on the world, rather than thrill to its beauty or be moved by its order or mystery. We need to show by the way we live that we believe this is God's world, that he is its creator and that he loves it. Creation is a good place to begin to appreciate the wonders of God that are all around you. The psalmist declares, 'The heavens are telling the glory of God: and the firmament proclaims his handiwork' (Psalm 19.1). God has given us this world; he has placed us in it, and like the rest of creation we are here to reveal his glory.

As well as being God's creation, this world is also the subject of his love. He did not make the world to be destroyed or despised; rather, even though it has been marred and disfigured, he seeks to redeem it. As God came down to earth in Jesus Christ, so we need to come down to earth – 'humus' and 'humility' are, after all, closely linked. For pilgrimage to get off to a good start it is necessary to acknowledge our relationship to the earth and to seek to approach the mystery

1

of God through what he has made. The Celtic Christians talked of three books of revelation: the New Testament, the Old Testament and creation. To understand the New Testament, you need some understanding of the Old Testament, and to understand the Old Testament you need some understanding of creation. If your attitude to the most humble parts of creation is wrong, your attitude to God will be wrong too, because if you say you don't love the world, how can you love its creator?

Sometimes, on pilgrimage, we will have to go slowly: it is not the distance we cover that matters so much as the discovery that we are walking on holy ground. Take your time now and think over these words by Teilhard de Chardin:

> All around us, to right and left, in front and behind, above and below, we have only to go a little beyond the frontier of sensible appearances in order to see the divine welling up and showing through . . . by means of all created things without exception, the divine assails us, penetrates us, moulds us. We imagined it as distant and inaccessible, whereas in fact we live steeped in its burning layers. *In eo vivimus.* As Jacob said, awakening from his dream, the world, this palpable world, which we were wont to treat with the boredom and disrespect with which we habitually regard places with no sacred association for us, is in truth a holy place, and we did not know it. *Venite adoremus.*[1]

However you look at life, you live in an amazing world. These days, we are privileged to be able to view the world from outer space. Images of our blue earth are truly awe-inspiring and humbling. In the entire universe, as far as we know, there is only one speck in the Milky Way that will sustain human life, and that is planet earth. This in itself is a cause for wonder. If the earth had been 15 per cent further away from the sun it would have been frozen; if it had been only 5 per cent nearer the sun, all water would have evaporated and it would have been a desert. But, in what is quaintly described as the 'Goldilocks Effect', it is 'just right', with a 'not too cold, not too hot' atmosphere, and the right ingredients within it for our survival. In many ways this unique world looks as if it was prepared for our arrival, and that is awesome.

When I was asked by a much-travelled friend, 'How far have you journeyed today?' I replied, 'Well in the last hour, about 64,000 miles.' Did you realize that at this very moment you're hurtling around the sun at 64,000 miles an hour? In one year you will travel 584 million miles to end up back where you started! And that is but a small part of your awesome journey.

When I was growing up my mother would often say to me, 'There really is no one like you,' or 'After God made you, he threw away the mould,' in response to which my father usually mumbled, 'Thank God.' I was never sure whether it was a compliment or a plea to conform. However, I have grown to appreciate more and more that each one of us is a special person, a one-off, a unique being. There really is no one like you in the whole universe and that in itself is awesome. The components that make up your body have been around since the beginning of creation, yet the trillions of drifting atoms have assembled in a pattern that has never existed before and never will again. This unique, special, never-to-be-repeated creation is you. No one else sees quite as you see, or hears quite as you hear. You can be recognized by your fingerprint, the pattern of blood vessels of your retina, your hair, your saliva and by samples of your DNA. Even if you are an identical twin, you have your own unique gifts to bring to the world, and the world will be the poorer without them. Again that is awe-inspiring.

You can choose to blend in with the crowd or to stand out – it's up to you. The danger is that we take things for granted and go by default with the flow, but isn't that what dead things and debris do? Only the living can move upstream. We are called to raise our sights, to break free of our self-imposed boundaries, to open our eyes to opportunities and our minds to adventure. And there is an even greater journey waiting, for we belong to more than the earth. Each of us is not merely a body but also a living soul. The world that we thought was beyond is actually here: heaven and earth are not separate but interwoven. God is in our midst, and the more we are aware of this, the more exciting our awesome journey becomes. It is a pilgrimage of life, and life in abundance. Come and explore with me!

On this journey, we need to discover a place that is special to us, one that creates a sense of wonder and awe. If we do not have such a place, we must set out to find one, as it is important that pilgrims carry such a sacred place within them when they travel. Angelus Silesius, the German mystic, writing in the seventeenth century said:

> Though Christ a thousand times
> In Bethlehem be born,
> If he is not born in you,
> You are still forlorn.

Our sacred place, where we encounter the incomprehensible, will be a place that is forever new. Travelling in depth as well as laterally is what distinguishes us from tourists. We do not merely clock up places we have been to and sights we have seen; we are also on a journey of being, an inward journey which cannot be easily catalogued or grasped but is a great adventure nonetheless.

Travel with me as we look at God's question to Adam, and how it relates to us now. Moving on to Abraham, we will explore ideas of life as pilgrimage and our awareness of, and openness to, others and the great other who is God. With Jacob, we will investigate if we have encountered a holy place that has opened our eyes to things invisible before. The story of Moses and the burning bush is concerned with someone whose heart was ablaze in the presence of God. Let us hear God's call to Moses as a call to us to move on in commitment and obedience: as St John Chrysostom said, 'It is not enough to leave Egypt; one must also enter the Promised Land.' With Elijah, we will explore times when we run out of resources and have no power to help ourselves. We will look at how God is our might and our salvation, someone we can only love because he first loved us; someone we cannot find unless he comes to us. When God calls to us in darkness and weakness, we need space and stillness in order to hear him. The record of Isaiah and the empty throne, which comes next, reveals how we react when our very foundations are shaken and talks of being emptied in order to be filled. We then look at the story Jesus told about 'The Prodigal Son', which is about faith and relationships and learning where true righteousness lies. Like the son, we need to re-turn, to repent, to discover love, acceptance and forgiveness. Moving on, St Paul writing from prison invites us and the Philippians to rejoice in the Lord, and to stop searching for what we already possess. On this awesome journey – which calls us to make new discoveries, to reach out, to show God's love – we need to know we are not on our own, for God is with us.

This life is meant to be a journey of delight, a pleasurable exploration into the wonders and mystery of the world and our own being. It is a journey of love: a journey with God and into God. The aim is to discover, in the words of Shakespeare from *Twelfth Night*, 'journeys end in lovers meeting'. Yet in another sense it is a journey without end, for it is concerned with eternal life and a relationship with God who is eternal.

I believe the Scriptures have much to say to us. The realities they speak about are the realities that we experience today. At the deepest level, our place in, and our relationship with, the world are much the same as those of our forebears. In a way, the Bible is the story of our life and our relationship with God. There is a lovely tale from Tanzania about a woman who was asked why she always carried the Bible around and never any other books. She replied, 'You can always read books; only the Bible reads you.'

A word or two about the use of the word 'awesome'. Words, like money, can suffer from devaluation, and if used inappropriately, their impact may be lessened. It might help to think of someone trying to understand an experience by reading about it rather than by doing it first hand: they don't really know what they're talking about. After all, you can't appreciate the thrill of being on a mountain top from reading maps, but only by climbing up there. In the Anglo-Saxon poem 'The Seafarer', the poet says of landsmen that they have no experience of his deprivations on the sea in winter:

> He who lives safely on land
> does not understand how I fare,
> careworn and cut off from my kinsmen
> on ice-cold ocean weathered winter
> in exile on an icy sea.

You have to have been in the grip of winter at sea to fully understand. Similarly, it's difficult to comprehend biblical encounters with holiness or glory – or, on a more human level, deep love – until we have experienced it. You can read love poems and encyclopaedia entries without truly knowing what love is. And there is a great division between those who have experienced the earthquake-like, life-changing thrill of something that is truly awesome and those who tend to use the word loosely to describe anything that excites them a little. The first group would own to a sense of awe, an awareness of the 'presence that disturbs', an entering into the 'cloud of unknowing'; the second would be quite oblivious to this dimension. God is with all of us but many are unaware of his presence. *The Awesome Journey* is an attempt to help us on our way.

At the end of each chapter there are exercises to enable you to put what you have read into practice, to enter into a time of quiet and reflect on your journey. The '5p exercise' is useful both for beginners and for those who want to think more deeply about the Bible. Each part of it can be described by a word beginning with the letter 'P': Pause, Presence, Picture, Ponder, Promise.

Pause It is important to stop and let go of what you are doing. We are usually so preoccupied that we do not have room for God to speak. Let God have a chance to enter your life. Remember, God speaks most clearly to those who can keep silent. Calm your mind and body.

Presence God is with you: you live in him and he lives in you. The reason for creating this space is not for knowledge, or peace, or even for love, but for God himself who comes to you. Affirm his presence. Remind yourself, no matter who you are, 'The Lord is with you.'

Picture what the fact of God's presence means for you. It can be good to use a verse or a passage of Scripture to help you see God at work, and to explore this with each of your senses, as if you were preparing to make a film of the text.

Ponder Think what the passage is seeking to say to you. The message will not always be comfortable; indeed, it should often challenge you. When God calls he also sends. Is there something God wants you to do through what you have been picturing?

Promise There is not always something to do, or change, but if there is, promise some sort of action. At the very least, you can undertake to affirm God's presence at various points throughout the day.

The '5p exercise' is a good way of experiencing life and Scripture in a deeper way. Because God is the creator of the world of nature and of grace, it is possible to see images of God at work through his world. In fact God speaks to us through his world, through our senses and through the material things around us.

God calls you out from where you are.
God calls you to adventure with him.
God calls you on an awesome journey.
Come!

Come where the division between sacred and
    secular disappears.
Come and discover that heaven and earth are one.
Come where God dwells in you and you in him.
Come!

Let your life become your prayer,
Let journeying be a walk with God.
Come on a discovery of yourself.
Come!

Get to know and love your own mysterious being.
Discover within yourself sacred space.
Enter into the time which is beyond time.
Come!

Then everywhere will be changed,
Every place will be transfigured,
Where God is known to be with you.
We will go on well-trodden paths and new ways.
You cannot come as an onlooker, that leaves you
    on the outside,
Though still you influence us, as we influence you.
Come and share the journey.
Come!

The God who calls you to the awesome journey
Is God who travels the road with you.
Make your home in him and welcome him.
Come!

1

೯ *Where are you?* ೯

Our birth is but a sleep and a forgetting:
The Soul that rises with us, our life's Star,
Hath had elsewhere its setting,
And cometh from afar:
Not in entire forgetfulness,
And not in utter nakedness,
But trailing clouds of glory do we come
From God, who is our home . . .[1]

The first book of the Bible is called Genesis (a Greek word for 'beginning'), as it opens with the words, 'In the beginning'. Before we set out on pilgrimage it is necessary to reflect on who we are. At the start of his life as a Christian, St Augustine prayed 'that I know me: that I may know thee'. His quest to know God was bound up with knowing himself, and we too need to understand ourselves in a way that is not solely intellectual, but rather involves appreciating our whole being. This kind of knowledge demands a deep loving relationship with oneself, with others and with God.

The first stage towards love is to know that we are loved and that we are loveable. And we surely are, for God created each one of us out of love and for his love. The Book of Lamentations, which could hardly be described as a book of joy, has this great gem: 'But this I call to mind, and therefore I have hope: The steadfast love of the LORD never ceases, his mercies never come to an end; they are new every morning; great is your faithfulness' (Lamentations 3.21–23). These words in their turn inspired John Keble to write:

New every morning is the love
Our wakening and uprising prove;
Through sleep and darkness safely brought,
Restored to life, and power, and thought.

And Thomas Obadiah Chisholm to rejoice:

Great is thy faithfulness! Great is thy faithfulness!
Morning by morning new mercies I see;
All I have needed Thy hand has provided,
Great is thy faithfulness, Lord, unto me![2]

We begin our pilgrimage assured of God's love for us. But many setting out on this quest, though they make a good start, then go off course. A midlife crisis is often about the sudden discovery that we have lost our way: we feel as if we have entered a dark wood or a grey fog and are no longer sure where we are going or to what purpose. Perhaps we have let other worldly things take over and become possessed by our possessions. Then there are the people I have met who have a genuine call and longing to proclaim God's love, but who have lost their vision because they are caught up in a mountain of paperwork, or email correspondence, or the arrangement of religious services. Attending to tasks like these is not wrong; indeed, it is often necessary. But it's dangerous when such activities take our focus away from what we should hold most dear. We need to check regularly to see if what we are doing is coming between us and our 'true' self, between us and our loved ones, between us and our God. If this seems to be the case for you today, be reassured that you can make a new start right now by remembering that 'new every morning is the love'.

When we read the Bible, we should find ourselves challenged about how we live, how we relate to others and how we relate to God. Time and again Scripture makes us think about who we are and where we are. In Genesis (to begin at the beginning), we are faced with the mystery of creation and our own being. There has been a tendency to describe creation as *ex nihilo*, that is, 'out of nothing', in order to emphasize the power of our Creator God. But I cannot fully go along with that. If you are created out of nothing, it is to nothing that you will return. Similarly, to say you are created 'out of dust and to dust you will return' may be to state a physical fact, but it fails to convey the hope of the resurrection or to recognize you are far more than a body. What I believe we need to understand is that we are created out of God, out of his own being, out of love and delight, and that it is to God's love and delight that we will return. A regaining of this vision of a world in which we live and move and have our being in a God who is ever present, will open our eyes to the reality we have very often lost. Living in this reality is the purpose of any true pilgrimage undertaken (in the words of many of the Celtic pilgrims) 'for the love of God'.

But we do tend to be distracted travellers! There is so much calling for our attention, so much that is pleasant to the eye and good to the taste. And as we can only learn as we go, it is easy to lose our bearings and wander off in the wrong direction. We may have access to a welter of information through smartphones, tablets and computers. However, these digital wonders, which help us extend our lives in many ways, should nonetheless come with a health warning. They have altered the way we interact with each other, the way we behave and the way we think. They have invaded most of our homes in the guise of technology, and encouraged us to feel we must be available at all times. English dictionaries now include the new word 'fomo', which is computer talk for the 'fear of missing out'. In one survey, 60 per cent of teenagers said they had to 'keep in contact' and were addicted to their smartphones. But their 'contact' with the world can in fact make them less directly connected: for example, they often send texts instead of speaking directly to one another, thus stunting the development of their interpersonal skills. Indeed, it is suggested that young people's personalities and imaginative capacities are being affected by constant use of media gadgets. It is very sad to hear someone boast about having many contacts and then realize that person spends much of his or her time in self-imposed isolation. Such people's knowledge of who they are is often low on the agenda. Instead, being overloaded with both good and evil information from their technological 'tree of knowledge', they have become lost, confused and reduced to living below their real capacity, when they might be growing into the person they could be. The promises of unknown gains have proved a snare: 'forbidden fruit' in the form of pornographic sites or ultra-violent movies can have a harmful effect on young lives for a long time, if not forever. Resonances with events in the Garden of Eden are all too apparent.

Let us reflect further now on Genesis. The first words in the Bible declare, 'In the beginning . . . God'. This is the base line of the creation story. It is not about how the world was made but about who made it; is not about the process but about the maker, the persona behind and within it all. The world is God's. God is in control. God is Almighty. God gives life. It is only when you are aware of these truths that you can live rightly in the world. Whether the world was made in six days or over billions of years is not the issue. The breathtaking fact is that there is a creator of all and that this creator delights in his world.

God gives the sky, the earth and the sea their names – not in the sense of assigning particular terms, but through bestowing on them the power to exist and their unique nature. From the smallest particle to the galaxies, the 'name' of something denotes its very essence. Without God it would have no *esse*, no being; it would not exist. Just as we give names to things or creatures that belong to us, in naming, God shows creation belongs to him.

'God created humankind in his own image, in the image of God he created them; male and female he created them' (Genesis 1.27). I can remember being fascinated at school by the chemical make-up of humans: a mixture of carbon, hydrogen, oxygen, nitrogen, a little calcium, a bit of iron and a spattering of other ordinary elements. I asked myself, is that all? I was delighted to find a more fun description that explained the average adult is made up of enough iron to make a four-inch nail, enough fat to make a few bars of soap, enough sugar to fill a sugar bowl, enough potassium to make a small explosion, enough phosphorus to manufacture 200 match heads and enough lime to whitewash a small shed. These constituents could be bought then for only a few pounds. However, I was aware that it took more than a few material

14

things to make a human being. Chemistry and physics told only part of the story.

Genesis chapter 2 adds more: 'Then the Lord God formed man from the dust of the ground, and breathed into his nostrils the breath of life: and the man became a living being' (Genesis 2.7). Here is something else. We are created of earthly elements – and the material facts helpfully remind us of our fragility and our limited time on this planet – but through the miracle of life, by the love of God, we arise from the dust of the earth a living being, a unique individual, made by God for his glory. In older translations of Genesis, the human being becomes a living soul through the breath of God. We do not possess a soul; we are a soul – body, mind and spirit. We may talk as if these are separate entities but they are all part of one being. Back at school, I abhorred the idea of dissecting frogs, because that was about analysing a dead thing that no longer swam or leapt or sang in the pond: it had lost a special part of its being – life! If we are not careful, analysis can do the same to poetry, to literature and to the human being: each has a totality, an otherness that cannot be fully captured. You may prefer the word 'person' to 'soul', but whichever word you use, it should help to remind you that you are a united being.

There is still more: 'God created humankind in his image; in the image of God he created them; male and female he created them' (Genesis 1.27).

We are the icon of God. On the computer screen, an icon serves to lead us to what is behind the icon, to what it represents. You may like to keep this in mind when you consider how we learn to approach the mystery of God: it is through the mystery of ourselves. When we discover that our own being, in all its fullness, is simply beyond our human understanding, we can begin to find within us – and to see in others – the mystery of God. This should fill us with awe but not arrogance. As icons we cannot treat each other with disrespect or neglect; rather we should celebrate the special nature each of us individually has been given, our 'otherness', which reflects the great 'other' who is God. If you fail to be yourself a light goes out on the earth, a light that only you can give. You can certainly learn from others and thus gain insights and expand your talents, but God does not want you to be a copy of another person. We each of us experience life in our own way and have our own story to tell, our own song to sing and our own love to share. This is our awesome journey, our pilgrimage of life. If we try to inhabit someone else's story, we simply become play actors and cease to be ourselves. This the Bible calls hypocrisy.

The Genesis story has a wonderful description of God coming to Adam and Eve 'in the cool of the day' or, as a more direct translation of the Hebrew says, 'in the wind of the evening'. I often notice a gentle breeze around sunset, which reminds me that God comes not in power but in gentleness, not to force us to give him our attention but to invite us to enjoy his presence. The question addressed to Adam and Eve, 'Where are you?' (Genesis 3.9), is primarily about humankind's relationship to God. He calls us by name and seeks a relationship with us, asks us personally to realize who we are, where we are, and the effects of what we are doing. If you are a stranger to yourself, it is not likely you will get to know the living God. Rather, as we've come to see, our way into the great other is through the mystery of ourselves. Without awareness and the paying of attention, we drift through life. Paying attention means attending to things or people and celebrating their existence. Our awareness of God most often comes through a deeper perception of what is around us. When we open our eyes to the beauty and diversity of our world and our hearts to the mystery of our being, we become aware of a 'beyond' in our midst. I often think of the opening lines of Gerard Manley Hopkins's poem 'God's Grandeur':

> The world is charged with the grandeur of God.
> It will flame out, like shining from shook foil.

God acts through the things of this world and yet he transcends all. Insensitivity to the world and to those around us makes us unresponsive to God. There can be no true worship or pilgrimage until the eyes are opened, and one of the major tasks of all leaders in the faith is to open the eyes of the blind. Rather than simply filling people with knowledge, we need to help them see and recognize themselves as individuals, for it is only when we are assured that we have a self to offer that we will be able to give this to others. God calls to every human, as he called to Adam, 'Where are you?' This can be scary if we have not really got to know ourselves and are afraid to emerge out of 'hiding'. All true relationships draw us out of our shell, but there is tension involved, as D. H. Lawrence shows in 'The Egotist':

> The only question to ask today, about a man or
>   a woman,
> is: Has she chipped the shell of her own ego?
> Has he chipped the shell of his own ego?
> They are all perambulating eggs

going: 'Squeak! Squeak! I am all things to myself,
yet I can't be alone. I want somebody to keep me
warm.'[3]

The call of God helps us grasp that life is far richer than we
ever dreamed. Much of the time we exist below par, failing
to be what we are created to be, a state which the Bible calls
sin. A sense of pilgrimage begins to come to the fore when
we feel called by God to arise to a more aware and loving
life. Our journey should lead us to know that we are loved,
and are loved with an everlasting love. Righteousness, or
right relatedness, is not about being perfect or about what
we may achieve, but about living in a right relationship
with God through his grace. This can only happen because
he calls us to himself. Heed the words of Psalm 95, 'Today
if you hear his voice harden not your heart'. We can hide
behind prayers and church services when God longs for us
to come to him personally. You may like to consider if the
words from 'The Hound of Heaven' by Francis Thompson
apply to you:

I fled Him, down the nights and down the days;
I fled Him, down the arches of the years;
I fled Him, down the labyrinthine ways
Of my own mind; and in the mist of tears
I hid from Him, and under running laughter.
Up vistaed hopes I sped;
And shot, precipitated,
Adown Titanic glooms of chasmèd fears,
From those strong Feet that followed, followed after.
But with unhurrying chase,
And unperturbèd pace,

Deliberate speed, majestic instancy,
They beat – and a Voice beat
More instant than the Feet –
'All things betray thee, who betrayest Me.'

Long ago, the prophet Hosea declared that God said: 'For I desire steadfast love and not sacrifice, the knowledge of God rather than burnt offerings' (Hosea 6.6). To learn this can be the beginning of the awesome journey, the beginning of the exciting pilgrimage of life. God does not leave us when darkness descends, as it does from time to time in every life; rather he remains with us, 'our light and our salvation'.

Exercises

1 Pray

Come I this day to the Father,
Come I this day to the Son,
Come I this day to the Holy Spirit powerful;
Come I this day with God,
Come I this day with Christ,
Come I this day with the Spirit of kindly balm.[4]

2 The 5p exercise

Pause Put out of your mind that you are too busy! You have time to stop, time to be still, time to give your mind a rest. Let your heart, your whole being, be open to what comes to you. Relax each part of your body in turn. Breathe gently and deeply. If your mind wanders, bring it back to the stillness, perhaps with the words, 'God, here am I'. This action alone is good for your being.

Presence God seeks you. God calls you. God is with you. It is not so much the case that you are waiting on God, as that he is waiting on you. God wants a living relationship with you. In the space you have created, seek to rest in him and to be open to him. If there appear to be no words, no presence, just be still and let God refresh you.

Picture Read Genesis 3.8–13. Try to picture the scene – it is one of confrontation and challenge. Adam and Eve have misused the great freedom they have been granted by choosing to follow their appetites and doing what they want. Becoming self-centred damages all their relationships and changes the world around them. God has to call and search for Adam because Adam is hiding due to feelings of guilt. His loving wife is now 'the woman you gave me', and Eve also seeks to place the blame for her choice elsewhere. Similarly, in the parable of the Prodigal Son, the father's elder son angrily refuses to call the prodigal his brother, referring to him instead as 'that son of yours'. When loving relationships break down, we debase ourselves, other people, the world and God. Yet even in these difficult times, God seeks us. Try to explore this idea by picturing God seeking you right now.

Ponder What are you hiding behind? The question to Adam is relevant to us all. We frequently hide from God and from the reality of what is happening in our lives. But though Adam turned away from God, God did not turn away from him. God still comes and abides with those who ignore him, disobey him, betray him, or are simply too busy to bother about him. And he comes not in condemnation but in love. God is always on speaking terms with us. He cares when we feel guilt and shame and longs to forgive us. Though we seek to fill ourselves, chasing pleasure and self-gratification, he knows that only he can provide real satisfaction. But he does not want us to shut out the world any more than he wants us to shut him out. Rather, God wants us to work with him and to let him work through us.

Promise you will turn towards the living God each day, and offer yourself to him as he gives himself to you.

3 Final prayer

Use these well-known words of St Augustine of Hippo:

Lord you have created us for yourself and our heart is restless until it rests in you.

2

ℳ *A divine discontent* ℳ

Alone with none but thee, my God,
I journey on my way:
What need I fear, when thou art near,
O King of night and day?
More safe I am within thy hand,
Than if a host did round me stand . . .

The child of God can fear no ill,
His chosen dread no foe;
We leave our fate with thee, and wait
Thy bidding when we go.
'Tis not from chance our comfort springs,
Thou art our trust, O King of kings.[1]

We are brought up with agendas, for agendas help us to get
things done. On our first day at school, we discover there
is a timetable for each day and soon we've settled into a
routine. We learn to plan our days, and some people are
confident enough to plan for a few years. Others of us are
all too aware that life itself is unpredictable – in both good
and bad ways – though unpredictability is never very easy
to deal with; 'for that we have insurance', said a friend!
Whatever our temperament, it is healthy once in a while to
leave behind the safety net of familiar and known ways and
to launch out into the unknown. Sometimes the impetus to

change is a reaction to dullness or boredom: we have an inner awareness that there is much more to life than what we are experiencing. Occasionally something upsets our normal routine, disturbs us out of our settled ways and points us to a way that is yet unknown. This is often when life can become a pilgrimage. The writer to the Hebrews says, 'By faith Abraham obeyed, when he was called to set out for a place that he was to receive as an inheritance; and he set out, not knowing where he was going' (Hebrews 11.8).

These words remind me of a story about the Royal Navy during the last war. The captain of a destroyer obeyed a command to take his vessel out of port on a mission. The sailors had charts, navigation aids and radar, but were unaware of their destination. In fact, no one on board knew where they were going, though they were well aware that the journey involved great risks. The officers' only agenda was to hear and obey. Each day the captain contacted base to report on the ship's progress and to receive instructions. When a task had been completed, he was given further instructions. This required great faith on his part in those who were ultimately directing operations. Those on the ship were travelling into the unknown, and truth be told, much of the journey of life is like this. We can never be certain where we are going.

Society today much admires those who have 'arrived', who have 'made it', by reaching some pinnacle of achievement in work or sport or the arts. I often respect such people myself. But we must realize that life does not stand still. Winners cannot bask in the glow of medals forever. We are all on the move, 'strangers and pilgrims upon the earth', as the Bible puts it. We are here to do something, but only for a while.

The bigger picture is that the world around us is full of mystery and wonder, and if we listen to our inner longings, we will sense a call to go on our own sacred journey, our personal pilgrimage into the unknown. I often meditate on the words of Hilary of Poitiers in his book, *On the Trinity*, which remind us that as long as we live, we have the potential to grow and change:

> When I began to search for the meaning of life, I was first attracted to the pursuit of wealth and leisure. As most people discover there is little satisfaction in such things, and a life orientated to the gratification of greed or killing of time is unworthy of our humanity. We have been given life in order to achieve something worthwhile, to make good use of our talents, for life itself points to eternity.

Abram (Abraham) is the first person we hear of in the Bible who is called into the unknown. He was born in the area of Ur of the Chaldees, situated near present-day Iraq, not far from Kuwait. Ur, with a population of around 250,000, was an important city, a place of learning where maths, astronomy, commerce and philosophy were all studied. Naturally, it drew people from far and wide. Abram's family unit lived around its edge as shepherds, possibly supplying some of the city's needs. However, many of the peoples and tribes in Europe and the Middle East were on the move at this time, probably because of changes in the climate: drought and famine were always great dangers. Abram's father, Terah, decided to move his tribal family, which included his son Abram and Abram's wife Sarai (Sarah), away from Ur. They journeyed around the edge of the Great Desert, passing Babylon and Nineveh, to settle in Haran in present-day south-east Turkey (Genesis 11.31).

When Terah died, Abram's younger brother, also called Haran, remained. Abram, however, believed God was calling him to move again; perhaps the land they had would not sustain both his and his brother's tribal families. In any case, 'Now the LORD said to Abram, "Go from your country and your kindred and your father's house to the land that I will show you. I will make of you a great nation, and I will bless you, and make your name great, so that you will be a blessing"' (Genesis 12.1–2). 'So Abram went, as the LORD had told him' (Genesis 12.4).

Not only does God's call fill us with awe, it disturbs our complacency and opens our eyes and hearts to new vistas. This is not easy to express, but I like these words of William Wordsworth:

> A presence that disturbs me with the joy
> Of elevated thoughts; a sense sublime
> Of something far more deeply interfused,
> Whose dwelling is the light of setting suns,
> And the round ocean and the living air,
> And the blue sky, and in the mind of man;
> A motion and a spirit that impels
> All thinking things, all objects of all thought,
> And rolls through all things.[2]

The presence of God is beyond description but it is not beyond our apprehension.

Encountering God in this intimate way is not always a comfortable experience: it can deeply disturb us, and by extension our routines and our agendas. The way God spoke to Abram would disrupt his tribe's settled way of life. Abram was not told the place he was to head for but only to 'go' into the unknown. When God calls, he offers no guarantees about tomorrow, and often the way is only revealed as we go along. But if we refuse, we will forever wonder what could have been. Abram truly didn't know where he was going, or how he would get there, or how long it would take, or even if he'd recognize when he'd arrived! All he knew was that God had called him. When I hear of a church anxious to keep things just as they have always been, I have to ask, is this a community on the move? Is it willing to let God disturb it, make it discontent with what it is and lead it out from a place of comfort and safety? Are we people who are willing to let God work similarly in our lives?

'So Abram went, as the LORD had told him' (Genesis 12.4). We witness here more than a journey from place to place: we see a journey of trust in God based on a personal relationship. Abram did not know what was ahead but he knew *who* was with him. God calls us to abandon our false gods and imagined securities and simply trust that he is with us and that he loves us. This is why the writer to the Hebrews says it is 'by faith' that Abram set out. Faith needs to be understood not as a set of beliefs or the ability to recite creeds, but as a living relationship with God. Later on under Moses, the people wandering in the wilderness got tired of journeying into the unknown and exchanged the glory of God for the image of an ox that ate grass (see Psalm 106.20). They sought something they could control in order to give them a sense of security (false idol though it was!). What might you be in danger of putting in God's place? A car that makes you feel powerful, a passion for sport, the affirmation

26

that comes with doing a responsible job well, a love of music, a quest for knowledge?

It is interesting how many Celtic Christians felt called to leave behind security and discover God in new journeys. They described themselves as *peregrini pro Dei amore*, or *peregrini pro Christi amore*, that is as 'pilgrims for the love of God', or 'pilgrims for the love of Christ'. This distinguished them from other *peregrini* – *peregrinus* means wanderer or traveller – who were more what we would think of as tourists. For these early Christian travellers, it was not wanderlust or the desire to see new places that made them leave their homes and monasteries, it was the call of the love of God and the desire to reveal it in their lives. In journeying along the road of life, they sought to deepen their own existence and become more closely aware of the presence of God. They would have agreed with these words by G. R. D. McLean:

> God our pilgrimage impels,
> To cross sea-waste or scale life-fells;
> A further shore,
> One hill brow more,
> Draws on the feet, or arm-plied oars,
> As our soul onward, upward soars.[3]

Every seeker is responding to a call to move on from unexamined daily living. It is often a yearning for fulfilment that urges us to seek to change not only our environment, but something within ourselves. We also need to recognize that God may be using our discontentment or restlessness to prompt us to look in new directions where we may be more aware of his presence and love around us.

Leaving the predictable for a while gives us a chance to move on with our lives. Feeling dislocated can be good for us! For example, we take our wrists for granted but if we dislocate a wrist we realize just how important it is to us. Dislocation can make us appreciate our home and our way of life, and who we are.

The following is said to be part of a sermon by St Columba and is typical of the attitude of the Celtic saints:

> God counselled Abraham to leave his own country and go in pilgrimage into the land which God had shown him, to wit the 'Land of Promise'... Now the good counsel which God had enjoined here on the father of the faithful is incumbent on all the faithful, that is to leave their country and their land, their wealth and their worldly delight for the sake of the Lord of the Elements, and go in perfect pilgrimage in imitation of Him.[4]

The Celtic saints, by living as strangers in a foreign land for the sake of Christ, became more conscious of the reality that they were citizens of another kingdom. By going away from home, they discovered that they were *Hospites Mundi*, 'Guests of the world'. This did not mean that they did not belong to or like the world; indeed they often showed great love for this place where God was 'The Lord of the Elements'. But they acknowledged that the world was for them a transitory dwelling, a place of perpetual change and only a part of their life. They recognized that they were pilgrims on life's journey, and (as we touched on earlier) that for pilgrimage to be real it has to be a moving experience. The outer journey is the visible sign that we are seeking to be changed in our inner being. More important than the place we are travelling to is our attitude, our intention and the engagement of our heart. We have to be personally involved in order to become more aware of God.

Here is some advice from medieval Ireland to those that go on pilgrimage to Rome (though you could change the destination to any place):

> Going to Rome? Going to Rome?
> It will bring much trouble, little gain.
> Your long journey could be in vain.
> The King you seek, will only appear
> If in your heart you brought him here.

It is no use just travelling to holy places, looking at scenery, taking photographs, collecting information or writing reports if we do not discover more about ourselves in the process. Pilgrimage often involves a reawakening of our senses as we become aware that the so-called ordinary has the capacity to become extraordinary; that nothing is truly secular for all is holy. Our knowledge of each other and of the world around us is bound up with our awareness of the mystery of creation and its creator. Caught up in the pressures of life, we can fail to see the simple beauty of a flower; we can fail to hear the call of a loved one or a plea for attention. But if the eyes of our hearts are open, our awesome journey will encompass new depths and heights of experience, and the great other who is God will be found within it and ourselves. To return to Gerard Manley Hopkins's poem 'God's Grandeur':

> The world is charged with the grandeur of God.
> It will flame out, like shining from shook foil;
> It gathers to a greatness, like the ooze of oil

Crushed. Why do men then now not reck his rod?
Generations have trod, have trod, have trod;

And all is seared with trade; bleared, smeared
    with toil;
And wears man's smudge and shares man's smell:
    the soil
Is bare now, nor can foot feel, being shod.

And for all this, nature is never spent;
There lives the dearest freshness deep down things...[5]

In Abram we are presented with a man of faith who was willing to risk an unknown future on God's leadership. Leaving Haran, he began his journey south to the place that God had called him, taking his wife, Haran's son Lot, a portion of the tribe and their possessions. When he came to Canaan, God reaffirmed his promise and provided more details (Genesis 12.7): 'To your offspring I will give this land.' In the first instance, Abram had just been given general assurances about the future and the blessing of God. But even now it was not straightforward. We are told there was a famine in the land (Genesis 12.10), and the extended family would have to go elsewhere in order to survive. There is tremendous irony in the story here: Abram had left everything to risk following God for a new future that God would show to him, and yet even though Abram had faithfully responded, God had led him to a land where there was nothing to eat! To follow God's way is no assurance of safety in this world.

This was one of many times that faithfulness to God would place Abram and his people at risk. Having travelled on to

Egypt because there was food there, the company later journeyed into the Negeb, the desert area in the south of Canaan.
There God reaffirmed his promise (Genesis 13.4) of vast
amounts of land and a great number of children, though
given that Sarah was still barren, this was a future possibility of which Abram yet had no evidence. God returned to
him again in a vision and promised, 'Do not be afraid, Abram,
I am your shield; your reward shall be very great' (Genesis
15.1). The story has no easy ending. Abraham, as God had
now renamed him, possessed no land when Sarah died and
had to go to the Hittites and pay over the odds for a single
cave in which to bury his loved one. He himself died with
one son at home – no great number of descendants, let alone
those numbering the stars of the heavens or the grains of
sand of the seashore. What had become of all that God had
promised Abraham? It would be nearly 800 years before his
descendants owned the land that he was promised and later
again before they would be seen as a great nation. But the
time would come. What mattered most was Abraham's faith,
his relationship with God. Whatever we possess we will leave
behind in the end on our journey to be with him forever.

Exercises

1 Pray

Disturb us, Lord, when we are too well pleased with
    ourselves,
when our dreams have come true
because we have dreamed too little,
when we have arrived safely
because we sailed too close to the shore.

Disturb us, Lord, when, with the abundance of things we
   possess,
we have lost our thirst for the waters of life;
having fallen in love with life,
we have ceased to dream of eternity
and in our efforts to build a new earth,
we have allowed our vision of the new heaven to dim.

Disturb us, Lord, to dare more boldly
to venture on wider seas
where storms will show your mastery;
where losing sight of land
we shall find the stars.
We ask you to push back
the horizons of our hopes;
and to push into the future
in strength, courage, hope and love.[6]

2 The 5p exercise

Pause This is how we should begin all times of prayer, in
stillness. Stop all activity, let your mind and body rest. Relax:
check your body for signs of tension and seek to ease what
you can; do not let troubled thoughts fill your mind. Make
space for something new to happen. Make room for God to
speak, for God to be able to touch your mind and heart. If
your mind wanders, bring it back and attend to the fact that
God is with you. You may like to affirm:

> Alone with none but thee, my God,
> I journey on my way:
> What need I fear, when thou art near,
> O King of night and day?

Presence God is with you. God never leaves you. In all your journeys God is present. Speak to God as you would to a friend. Enjoy his presence. Every time your mind wanders, affirm, 'You Lord are here: you are with me.' Seek to wait upon God, as God has waited upon you.

Picture Read Genesis 12.1–9. Picture the calling of Abram and his wife. At 75, Abram was at the stage when most people would think their time of adventure was over. He was well settled, comfortable and prosperous. And then God urged him to leave the relative safety of his surroundings and move into the unknown. No doubt Sarah had something to say! It could have been, of course, that the old couple were given a jolt to change their circumstances by something like an impending famine. Try and picture them setting out into the unknown with hearts of faith. Countless people in our modern world are having to leave their homes and become refugees, aliens in a foreign land, and undertake journeys often fraught with danger and hostility.

Ponder Think how you would have reacted to a call such as Abram had. 'By faith Abraham obeyed when he was called to set out for a place that he was to receive as his inheritance; and he set out, not knowing where he was going' (Hebrews 11.8). Abram knew that wherever he travelled, God would be with him. He had a living relationship with God. Do you perceive God's call in what is happening to you today? How alive is your relationship with him?

Sometimes a call is less easy to perceive: it may come quite subtly through a discontent with the present, and an awareness that life and our surroundings, if not the world, could be better than they are. But there is always an immediacy about the call, and once heard, it should not be put off. We are asked to respond like Isaiah and say, 'Here am I, Lord, send me.' Having expressed that, it is important to ask God for guidance as to whether we are really hearing him summoning us, or if we are responding to a whim or a desire of our own.

Promise Those whom God calls he sends. The call to move out and have an adventure is of its nature exciting. Too often after the call nothing happens. Promise to keep at least a little of each day open to God and say each day, 'Here am I, Lord, send me.' Offer yourself in his service.

God, who called our Father Abraham to journey
   into the unknown,
Who led him, protected him, and loved him, be
   known to us on our journey through life.
May our eyes see you in all whom we meet.
May we learn to laugh in your presence:
To rejoice in you and your faithfulness to us
For as you blessed Abraham we are blessed by you,
You are our Father, we are your children,
With you we are on our way to the Promised Land.

3

ꙥ *The other in our midst* ꙥ

> I saw a stranger at yestere'en.
> I put food in the eating place,
> drink in the drinking place,
> music in the listening place,
> and in the sacred name of the Triune
> He blessed myself and my house,
> my cattle and my dear ones,
> and the lark said in her song,
> often, often, often,
> goes the Christ in the stranger's guise.[1]

The LORD appeared to Abraham by the oaks of Mamre, as he sat at the entrance of his tent in the heat of the day. He looked up and saw three men standing near him. When he saw them, he ran from the tent entrance to meet them, and bowed down to the ground. He said, 'My lord, if I find favour with you, do not pass by your servant. Let a little water be brought, and wash your feet, and rest yourselves under the tree. Let me bring a little bread, that you may refresh yourselves, and after that you may pass on – since you have come to your servant.' So they said, 'Do as you have said.' And Abraham hastened into the tent to Sarah and said, 'Make ready quickly three measures of choice flour, knead it, and make cakes.' Abraham ran to the herd, and took a calf, tender and good, and gave it to the servant, who hastened to prepare it. Then he took curds and milk and the calf that he had prepared, and set it before them; and he stood by them under the tree while they ate.

They said to him, 'Where is your wife Sarah?' And he said, 'There, in the tent.' Then one said, 'I will surely return to you in due season, and your wife Sarah shall have a son.' And Sarah was listening at the tent entrance behind him. Now Abraham and Sarah were old, advanced in age; it had ceased to be with Sarah after the manner of women. So Sarah laughed to herself, saying, 'After I have grown old, and my husband is old, shall I have pleasure?' The LORD said to Abraham, 'Why did Sarah laugh, and say, "Shall I indeed bear a child, now that I am old?" Is anything too wonderful for the LORD? At the set time I will return to you, in due season, and Sarah shall have a son.' But Sarah denied, saying, 'I did not laugh'; for she was afraid. He said, 'O yes, you did laugh.'   (Genesis 18.1–15)

It was by watching David Lean's 1962 British film, *Lawrence of Arabia*, that I got an insight into what it is like to look across the desert in the shimmering heat. Nothing seems to be of any substance; there are simply dancing spots of colour. Then in one dramatic moment, when Lawrence (played by Peter O'Toole) and an Arab are at a water well, there appears in the distant blue haze a quivering darkness. It is small to start with, but as it grows nearer, an aura can be discerned around it. At last the object takes on a recognizable shape. It is a man on a camel: the owner of the well, Ali, played by Omar Sharif. He is a solid being and very commanding.

This scene made me think of Abraham having his siesta in the heat of the day. He has pitched his tent near the oaks of Mamre and sits in the shelter of the entrance, gazing out at the desert. Perhaps he too looks into a quivering blue distance where figures dance before his eyes – figures, appearing insubstantial, which slowly take shape and become men. We can deduce from the fact that they are travelling in the heat of the day that they have an important purpose to fulfil. Abraham runs to meet them and bows to the ground. With true Bedouin hospitality, he offers them rest, shelter, food and refreshment. He offers to go and get water and to wash their feet. Then he offers them food – and he certainly does not stint! If you look at the menu, you will see that there was a whole calf, bread, milk and curds for just the three of them. As was the custom, the master of the house looked on while his guests ate.

The conversation that takes place concerns things only the Lord knows of, and it seems clear that he is seeking Abraham's attention through this call on his hospitality. Sarah's laughter at the ridiculous promise that she will conceive a child in her old age may have been inaudible, and she is quick to deny it when challenged, but the Lord makes it clear that he knows she is laughing at what seems an impossibility in her eyes. Earlier we are told that Abraham fell on his face and laughed for the same reason, and due to this he is told to call the child Isaac, meaning 'laughter' (Genesis 17.17, 19). Laughter is mentioned again when Isaac

37

is born and Sarah says, 'God has brought laughter for me; everyone who hears will laugh with me' (Genesis 21.6–7). The presence of God and his angels in a life is often revealed through an appealing light-heartedness and the ability to laugh at oneself.

We have a natural tendency to limit God by our own limited sight, but he challenges us: 'is anything too wonderful for the LORD?' (Genesis 18.14). Abraham and Sarah are asked to have faith, to enter into the unknown as they continue journeying with God. Their visitors are obviously men, but we know they are also messengers from God, for the chapter begins by stating that the Lord appeared (Genesis 18.1), and at the beginning of chapter 19, two of the men are described as angels. It would seem the Scriptures want us to view this encounter on more than one level. Are we dealing with men or angels or with the Lord? To say the visitors were three men is not to ask us to accept a lower idea of angels, but to see human beings raised to their true height.

If you believe that each one of us is an icon, an image of God, it follows that we have access to God through each other. Every human being has the potential to be an angel, not only in the sense of being a messenger, but also in that of drawing others into a more profound awareness of God's presence. Let's go back to those icons on your computer: if you click on one of those little images, you gain access to sites you could not see before. It is not too much of a stretch of the imagination to perceive that if we give our undivided attention to another human being, we can be led into greater depths. The letter to the Hebrews picks this up with the words: 'Do not neglect to show hospitality to strangers, for by doing that some have entertained angels without knowing it' (Hebrews 13.2). Saul, who became St Paul, was thunderstruck on the Damascus road when he heard Jesus say to him, 'Saul, Saul, why do you persecute me?' (Acts 9.4). Jesus had already told his own followers how in caring for the stranger, the naked, the sick and the prisoner we meet him: 'Just as you did it to one of the least of these who are members of my family, you did it to me' (Matthew 25.31–46, note especially verses 40 and 45). Mahatma Gandhi, the father of the Indian nation, who inspired movements for civil rights and freedom across the world, said, 'If you do not find God in the next person you meet it is a waste of time looking for him further.'

I heard a story of a monastery where the monks were not at peace with each other or with God. They were often impatient, angry or jealous. Then one day the Guest Master answered a knock on the door. A visitor stood in the shadows and whispered, 'One of you is the Christ.' Turning away, he was gone in a moment. The Guest Master related this incident to a meeting of the brothers later that morning, and afterwards, everyone left in silence. They had much to think about. Slowly the whole monastery was transformed, as the monks learned to deal with each other in a new way. Peace descended as they sought to be aware of the Christ.

For many in our world, the way into God's presence is through giving service – in attending to, caring for and loving others. When I was at college, spending time seeking to know God, I found this was not something I could do in a vacuum. God speaks to us through the world he has made and through the people that come to us. It was during this period that I learnt the following lines:

I sought my God
My God I could not see.
I sought my soul
My soul eluded me.
I sought my brother
And I found all three.

Prayer, study and silence are important, but so too is the fact that God is present in our encounters with others. St Martin of Tours met a poor beggar under a bridge, and because the man was suffering from the cold, cut his cloak in half and shared it with him. Later Martin dreamed of Christ with a half cloak in his hand saying, 'Look what Martin, who is still a catechumen, has given me today.' There are many such stories concerning the saints.

St Francis, who is seen as a lover of nature, had to over-come his own repulsion when faced with a leper. He was aware he could not ignore this man, for the leper needed to know that though society scorned him, he was not scorned by God. Francis took the leper into his embrace and held him in loving care, and as he held the leper, he knew he embraced the Christ and Christ in return embraced him. The poor rejected man had brought Francis before the great other who is God.

St Christopher, who became the patron saint of travellers, was someone who wanted to meet God personally. After much searching, Christopher was persuaded that in assist-ing others he would serve his God, so he took on the task of helping travellers at a dangerous ford. On one occasion, he was confronted with a child who needed to cross when the waters were high. Christopher waded into the water and raised the boy higher as the waters got deeper. After a considerable struggle, the pair reached the other bank. Christopher set the child down while he proceeded to dry himself, and suddenly became aware that the boy had disappeared. Christopher was convinced he had carried the Christ child. Even though the boy had another name and had run off home, Christopher knew he had met with Christ. Such encounters reveal more at work than just a meeting between humans. Meditate on these words by Thomas Ogletree:

> Strangers have stories to tell which we have never heard before, stories which can redirect our seeing ... Their stories invite us to see the world from a novel perspective ... The stranger does not simply challenge or subvert our assumed world of meaning, she may enrich, even transform that world.[2]

We live in a world where we often avoid encounters and are suspicious of strangers. Instead of hospitality, we may be dismayed to find ourselves experiencing a sense of hostility. The Abraham story reveals the results of hostility in the next chapter of Genesis, when two of the angels go to Sodom. They are welcomed by Lot and invited to stay. But before they lie down for the evening, the men of Sodom demand the men be brought out and act aggressively towards them. It is suggested that the hospitality of Lot saves him and his family and that it is this act of hostility that causes Sodom to be destroyed.

Let me repeat the quotation from the letter to the Hebrews, which we would all do well to follow! Though this can be hard to do at times, it is good advice:

Do not neglect to show hospitality to strangers, for by doing that some have entertained angels without knowing it. (Hebrews 13.2)

Exercises

1 Pray

Give me to recognize in others, Lord God, the radiance of your own face. The irresistible light of your eyes, shining in the depth of things . . . Grant me now to see you above all in the most inward, most perfect, most remote levels in the souls of my brothers and sisters.[3]

2 The 5p exercise

Pause Take a breather. Sit as comfortably as possible; check over your body and your mind for signs of tension. Seek to be at ease. Now simply be aware of yourself breathing: every intake is a renewing of your body; every exhalation makes this possible. Be at rest. You are making space for new things to happen.

Presence Affirm that God is with you: you do not have to seek him. Give your attention to him and rejoice in his love for you. You may like to use the following:

> Open my eyes that I sleep not in death
> Open my eyes to your presence
> Open my heart to your love
> God you are here and with me
> God you are here
> God you are
> God.

Picture Read Genesis 18.1–15. Try and capture the scene as if you are planning to make a film. Use your five senses to build up a picture of this meeting. Visualize the men coming out of the shimmering desert and think of Abraham's reactions and the respect that he shows towards them. See him bow down and wash their feet. Capture the conversation and the laughter, as they eat and drink. They have a message for Abraham and Sarah. Can you capture the importance of what is said and why?

Ponder If the men were only desert travellers, this encounter would hardly warrant recording. But they were more. What sort of image do you have of angels? Are you able to imagine the reality of this image and yet see angels as messengers of God? If we restrict our ideas to large fairy-like creatures with wings dressed in white, we will lose sight of the truth. In every encounter we can learn of God's presence as communicated through those we meet. How do you see this thought affecting the way you deal with others?

Promise to be less hostile towards strangers and more hospitable. Seek to see God in others and to bring God to others. Be an angel!

4

✂ *Liminal places* ✂

Not where the wheeling systems darken,
And our benumbed conceiving soars! –
The drift of pinions, would we hearken,
Beats at our own clay-shuttered doors.

The angels keep their ancient places –
Turn but a stone and start a wing!
'Tis ye, 'tis your estrangèd faces,
That miss the many-splendoured thing.[1]

In the television series, *Holy England*, Rabbi Lionel Blue said: 'Of all the places in Holy England, Holy Island is the holiest of all.' He was echoing words of Alcuin, who was a Northumbrian and adviser to Charlemagne. After the Viking invasion of the island in 793, Alcuin described it as the most venerable place in Britain. I was privileged to work there for many years. Yet, caring for the island, the people and the church was no sinecure. Many a night I fell asleep exhausted! The busyness, the coming and going of visitors and my crowded agenda often squeezed out any awareness of holiness. Even the church services were in danger of being said by rote. One crowded day in August, when bus loads were turning up by the dozen, I felt I had had enough. It was midday, and I had been in the church for over four hours. The place was thronging, with an elderly group eating their sandwiches at the back of the nave, and children playing by a side altar. I wanted to escape; I was missing 'the many-splendoured thing'.

Then a group of young people strode in. They made straight for the front pews on either side of the main aisle and almost filled four rows. After a deep bow to the east, acknowledging God's presence, all the youngsters knelt except for one pretty young woman who stood with her arms raised in prayer. An expectant stillness descended on the whole church. The air began to tingle. The children were the first to sense the change and became absolutely still and quiet. The group at the back stopped eating their sandwiches and bowed their heads. All were being touched by something deep and mysterious, a strange power at work that you could actually feel with your whole being.

After a while, the young woman lowered her arms. The whole group then arose, made another bow and went out. They left a hushed building and an awareness that something special had just taken place. How long the vibrant silence lasted I could only guess. Maybe it was two or three minutes, but it was touched with eternity.

Following the group out, I enquired about their visit. Sadly, as I should have been able to guess, they were not from the UK. In fact, only one young man could speak English. His sentences were carefully formed and thoughtful. 'We are from Slovakia. As Christians, we have a new freedom. To celebrate our new liberty, we sought one of the holiest places we had heard of and came to give thanks to God. Our pilgrimage is one of thanksgiving.' Needless to say, I was deeply moved by the directness and simplicity of his statements. It was his next sentence that caused me much joy and amusement.

'I hope that we did not disturb anyone.' I could only take his hand and say, 'Thank you. I believe that you have disturbed us all by revealing the presence that is ever with us. God bless you all on your journey.'

I was so fortunate to live in such a holy place. Though I would never see those young people again, what they had done would remain with me forever. Without words they had introduced all of us who were present to the holy and the mysterious. As they rejoiced in God's presence, they helped others to be more aware that 'The Lord is in this place.' More of us discover that presence through circumstances and encounters than through sermons and words.

We will take up this thought again later in the chapter. For now, let's return to the Bible, which we have already observed does not paint a rosy picture of people but rather shows how God works through them in real situations. The first family we encounter has a feud going on, which results in Cain killing his brother Abel. Another case of sibling rivalry is that between Abraham's grandchildren, Esau and Jacob.

Abraham's son Isaac and his wife Rebekah have had twins. In the ancient world, the birth of twins was always a danger-ous affair, not least in physical terms, and we are told that the twins struggled within Rebekah. There is a tradition in Judaism that Jacob was striving to be first, but in fact Esau emerged first from the womb and thus, by right of primo-geniture, would inherit by far the most from his father. The struggle as they were born almost together – the first child all red and hairy, the second grasping his brother's heel – would continue in the early part of their lives. Esau's name possibly means 'rough' or 'hairy' in the original Hebrew; Jacob's is thought to come from the word for 'heel', or that for 'deceiver', both being very close in sound. Indeed, in his early life Jacob turns out to be quite a heel and a deceiver!

We first hear of this character trait when the twins are young men. Esau, who as a hunter has been out all day in the open country, comes back 'dying of hunger'. Jacob, who is more often to be found around the home area – though we must remember that all the people were tent dwellers and keepers of herds of sheep and goats – says he will trade him a dish of red lentils for Esau's birthright. He persuades his brother to give up his future inheritance in exchange for a small but immediately available satisfaction. We who are willing to sacrifice the eternal for present gratification should not be surprised at this (see Genesis 25.29–34).

The next time we hear of Jacob's cheating is when his father Isaac is old and blind. Isaac wants to bless his first-born and so hand on the promises of God. He calls Esau and sends him to hunt game and provide from this some savoury food. But then we get a little insight into the divisions and favouritism within this very ordinary family. The father naturally favours his firstborn, Esau. The mother prefers the company of Jacob, and the two enter into cahoots. Rebekah gets Jacob to kill a young kid for her so she can make a savoury dish for Isaac. Then she helps Jacob dress in Esau's best clothes, so that he smells of the flock, and then makes him feel hairy, by putting the skin of the kid on his hands and the smooth part of his neck. With the food prepared, Jacob goes to his father, who mistakes him for Esau, and thus gains his father's blessing, which once given cannot be revoked (Genesis 27.1–29).

Almost immediately after this, Esau returns and brings in the savoury food. The elder son and his father discover they have been deceived! Esau is furious; filled with hate for Jacob, he plans to kill him just as soon as Isaac dies. Rebekah advises Jacob to flee at once and make his way back to her brother Laban in Haran, but before he goes, she persuades Isaac to send him away with a blessing and directions to marry among his kinsfolk (Genesis 27.30—28.1).

It seems that all Jacob's scheming has gone awry as he turns away from his home, his heritage and the Promised Land. There has been no mention of God in the younger son's life up to this point, and it would seem he has been preoccupied with triumphing over his brother and seeking worldly gains. But now, leaving Beersheba and heading towards Haran, he is detached from his family and familiar surroundings. He arrives at a 'certain place' at the edge of the Promised Land as the sun has set and stops for the night. Taking a stone of the place, he puts it under his head and lies down in the place. In the Jewish tradition, 'the place' is one of the names of God, and it is repeated three times in this verse (Genesis 28.11) to emphasize its importance. The place is where God is, but Jacob, all unaware, is asleep in the dark, oblivious of the other world that is woven into this one.

But here on the edge of the Promised Land, God makes himself known. In a dream, Jacob sees a ladder set up on the earth which reaches to heaven. On the ladder, the angels of God are ascending and descending. And the Lord stands beside him. Jacob is not alone on his journey, for the Lord is there and he reveals himself as 'the LORD, the God of Abraham your father and the God of Isaac; the land on which you lie I will give you and to your offspring' (Genesis 28.13). The covenant with Abraham and Isaac is confirmed once again, and Jacob is to be the one in whom the promise is fulfilled. But more, God assures Jacob, 'Know that I am with you and will keep you wherever you go, and will bring you back to this land' (Genesis 28.15). Jacob is given the promise of the presence and the protection of God. When he awakes out of sleep it is into a new vision of the world: 'Surely the LORD is in this place – and I did not know it!' And full of awe, wonder and fear, he says, 'How awesome is this place! This is none other than the house of God, and this is the gate of heaven' (Genesis 28.16–17).

The stone Jacob has used for a pillow, he now sets up as a memorial. It is to stand as a reminder that the Lord is in this place and that the Lord's presence and protection are at hand. Jacob renames the place itself and calls it 'Bethel', that is, 'House of God' (see Genesis 28.10–22).

At this time in history, many standing stones were erected as memorials, guides and signs of a beyond in our midst. I have stood by standing stones on the edges of lochs, on the high moorlands and in pasture land, and can understand why earlier peoples would have wanted to acknowledge a presence in such places. There are moments – often fleeting – when we are aware that heaven and earth are one, and that the Lord is beside us. If we manage to step aside from our preoccupations, hurry and worry, we may grasp the depth and importance of such experiences, which are hard to put into words. God shows himself to us through earthly things, through matter, yet he remains transcendent. When we acknowledge that God is present in the world and that he speaks to us through creation, seeing becomes more than mere observation. We can no more fully explain what we perceive than we can capture it on camera. That it is something real and true will be revealed in the difference it makes to our lives.

'Then Jacob woke from his sleep' (Genesis 28.16). Sadly many of us are hardly more than half awake as we journey through life. David Thoreau, in his book, *Walden*, said, 'To be awake is to be alive. I have never yet met a man who was quite awake.' In the same way, St Cuthbert said after his vision of angels, 'O, what wretches we are. We are so dull and full of sleep that we miss the glory that is all about us. If only we could open our eyes.' When we are fully awake, we will perceive the ordinary as extra-ordinary, and it will inspire in us wonder and awe, as illustrated in the story of *The Little Prince*:

> 'The men where you live', said the little prince, 'raise five thousand roses in the same garden – and they do not find in it what they are looking for!'
>
> 'They do not find it,' I replied.
>
> 'And yet what they are looking for could be found in one single rose or a drop of water.'
>
> 'That is true,' I said.
>
> And the little prince added: 'But the eyes are blind: one must look with the heart.'[2]

'One day when the bluebells were in bloom,' Gerard Manley Hopkins entered in his diary for 18 May 1870, 'I wrote the following. I do not think I have seen anything more beautiful than the bluebell I have been looking at. I know the beauty of our Lord by it.'[3] This kind of attention involves the heart, and indeed the whole being. It is an act of love, beyond words. We can only get an inkling of its wonder if we have had a similar experience.

I can remember leaving the dark of the coal mine after working the nightshift and entering into a bright sunlit day. A few of us got on our bikes and started speeding home for breakfast. As we drew near the bottom of a hill, I glimpsed a sea of blue in the nearby wood. My workmates continued their journey, but I had to turn aside. Leaving my bike by the verge of the road, I entered into the stillness of that place and was moved by the beauty of the bluebells. This sea of flowers not only provoked a sense of awe and wonder, it also conveyed something of the glorious power that fills our world. I wanted to capture its essence; to share it with my mother who was ill at home. So I took off my pit hat and filled it with bluebells, placed it safely in my bag and cycled back to our house. Once there, I found I could not explain the beauty of those flowers or what it had made me feel. Indeed, I was a little sad to see my offering looked rather limp and droopy. Yet my mother was overjoyed at the gift. Much later I would read some more words from a sermon preached in 1881 by Gerard Manley Hopkins:

All things, there, are charged with love, are charged with God and if we know how to touch them give off sparks and take fire, yield drops and flow, ring and tell of him.[4]

A liminal place ('liminal' meaning 'threshold') is a place of transition to another world. It is where the eyes of the heart are opened and we know 'the Lord is here'. We all need such places, for without them we live in a sphere that is too narrow, where we will be in danger of ceasing to marvel at who we are and of taking for granted the mysteries that are about us. And if we do those things, how can we hope to be aware of the greater mystery of God and the wonder of our God-filled creation? Teilhard de Chardin expresses this dilemma well in *Le Milieu divin*:

> All around us, to right and left, in front and behind, above and below, we have only to go a little beyond the frontier of sensible appearances in order to see the divine welling up and showing through . . . By means of all created things without exception, the divine assails us, penetrates us, moulds us. We imagined it as distant and inaccessible, whereas in fact we live steeped in its burning layers. *In eo vivimus*. As Jacob said, awakening from his dream, the world, this palpable world, which we were wont to treat with the boredom and disrespect with which we habitually regard places with no sacred association for us, is in truth a holy place, and we did not know it. *Venite adoremus*.[5]

The material and the spiritual are inseparable. The visible world of matter and the invisible world of spirit are interwoven; they are not two worlds but one. We all belong to both, here and now, and recognizing this is vital to our well-being. There is, of course, a life beyond this world, beyond what we call death. But if life is eternal we are already in it! (We do not have to wait until we die physically to experience eternity, though we may have a clearer vision and a fuller life later on.) Let's seek to live in the eternal now! Try to make yourself at home in the world and at home with God. To do this you may have to discover at least one holy place: somewhere that for you is vibrant with the presence of God. This may be a church, but it does not need to have the designation 'holy'. What about a room in your house, a spot on the high moorland, or a corner of your work place?

God is in all these places and, indeed, wherever you go. Find a space which represents for you a stepping stone into a larger world. It is only when you have such a spot that you will begin to see that everywhere has the potential to be a 'thin place', a location (such as the Isle of Iona) which seems conducive to our being more than usually aware of the presence and holiness of God. Ironically, we are often in search of what we already have. It is not that God is absent from where we are: it is we who are absent from God. We need to attend to him wholeheartedly.

Exercises

1 Pray

Lord, open my eyes, lest I sleep in death
Open my eyes to the wonder of creation
Open my eyes to the mystery of our universe
Open my eyes to your presence in all things
Open my eyes to know you are beyond all things
Open my heart to your love for me and for the world.

2 The 5p exercise

Pause Seek to unwind in the presence of God. Relax. Let go of all tension, make sure you are sitting comfortably. Breathe gently and deeply. Quietly wait upon God, knowing he is with you. To keep your mind at rest you may like to say, 'The Lord is in this place.'

Presence Affirm that God is with you. Enjoy being with him. Make space for him in your life. You cannot make God come for he is already with you. Open your heart to him. Do not fill all this time with words, just seek to rejoice in his presence and love and leave God space to speak to you.

Picture Read Genesis 28.10–22. Picture Jacob at the end of a trying day in which he has left home, possibly in disgrace. He has deceived his father and cheated his brother. His own brother is planning to kill him, so no doubt it is no longer safe to be at home or in the land of promise. At the moment he is alone and the future is daunting. Night is drawing near and the darkness will descend quickly. Jacob takes a stone for a pillow and lies down to sleep. Visualize his dream. See the ladder set between heaven and earth. The two are one, with angels coming and going all the time. We are all both receiving messages from God and messengers of God, if our hearts are in tune with him. Do not try to analyse, but visualize instead. God is there. Hear him say to Jacob: 'Know that I am with you and will keep you wherever you go . . . I will not leave you.' Be with Jacob as he awakens, overawed. Life will never be the same again, for God is with him and in the world. This is a life-changing event, never to be forgotten. Listen to Jacob as he says: 'Surely the Lord is in this place – and I did not know it . . . How awesome is this place! This is none other than the house of God, and this is the gate of heaven.' Jacob wants to do something to express his feelings. He renames the place Bethel. For him it is a holy place, a liminal place. Stay with Jacob for a while as he sets up a standing stone and try to enter into his feelings.

Ponder It was not under the best of circumstances that Jacob left home. The act of moving away from familiar surroundings and going away on his own may have opened up new sensitivities. Dislocation often makes us more aware. We can hardly think that Jacob deserved this vision, so far from perfect was he, but God is always gracious. God comes to us, God is with us, whether we deserve it or not. 'Jacob woke from his sleep' – had he been in that sleep all his life? – and out under the stars, his eyes were opened. He saw there was a greater depth to the world and to life than he had known. Meditate again on the words of Francis Thompson, with whom we began this chapter:

> O world invisible, we view thee,
> O world intangible, we touch thee,
> O world unknowable, we know thee,
> Inapprehensible, we clutch thee.
>
> . . .
>
> The angels keep their ancient places –
> Turn but a stone, and start a wing!
> 'Tis ye, 'tis your estrangèd faces,
> That miss the many-splendoured thing.

Have your eyes been opened? Do you see beyond the obvious? Can you say, 'Surely the Lord is in this place'? Quietly affirm that, though unseen, God is ever near. Know that God will not leave you or forsake you. That you are in his heart and he dwells in you. Have you been going on pilgrimage to seek what you already possess? What are you looking for? Heed these words:

> You are seeking God, dear sister, and he is everywhere. Everything proclaims him to you, everything reveals him to you, everything brings him to you. He is by your side, over you, around you and within you. Here

is his dwelling and yet you still seek him. Ah! You are searching for God, the idea of God in his essential being . . . But he will never disclose himself in that exalted image to which you vainly cling.[6]

Promise to affirm the presence of God in this day and in each day of your life. Do this at regular intervals by speaking directly to him. You may like to repeat:

You Lord are here:
You are in my heart,
I am in your heart,
Your presence is love.

3 Final prayer

Awaken me Lord
To your light,
Open my eyes
To your presence.

Awaken me Lord
To your love,
Open my heart
To your indwelling.

Awaken me Lord
To your life,
Open my mind
To your abiding.

Awaken me Lord
To your purpose,
Open my will
To your guiding.[7]

5

∝ *Hearts on fire* ∝

The Bright Field
I have seen the sun break through
to illuminate a small field
for a while, and gone my way
and forgotten it. But that was the pearl
of great price, the one field that had
the treasure in it. I realize now
that I must give all that I have
to possess it. Life is not hurrying

on to a receding future, nor hankering after
an imagined past. It is the turning
aside like Moses to the miracle
of the lit bush; to a brightness
that seemed as transitory as our youth
once, but is the eternity that awaits you.[1]

The Moses story seems at first to be a folk tale with a happy ending. The child was born into a loving family but his people had become aliens in Egypt. After being held in some respect by one Pharaoh, due to Joseph, they had come to grief under another and were now being used as slave labour. The sheer number of these Hebrews began to worry Pharaoh, and the simple remedy, he decided, was ethnic cleansing: he would have all the newly born male Hebrew children killed.

Moses's mother hid her tiny son from the moment he was born. When she began to feel it was no longer safe to do so, she put him in a little wicker basket, made watertight, and placed this among the reeds of the Nile. When the Pharaoh's daughter came to bathe in the river, she discovered the baby, rescued him and took him to the palace to be brought up in the royal household. But through subterfuge, he was also cared for by his own mother, who no doubt passed on to her son the stories of the Hebrews.

It was seeing his own people suffer under forced labour – and the beating of one by an Egyptian – that aroused the grown Moses to anger. He killed the Egyptian, but this, his first attempt to come to the aid of the Hebrews, misfired. The next day when he saw two Hebrews fighting and tried to intervene, they asked, 'Who do you think you are?' – they did not see him as one of their own. And though Moses thought no one knew about the incident with the Egyptian, news of it had spread, even to the ears of Pharaoh.

Now, as Pharaoh sought to kill Moses, it became clear that he no longer belonged to the Egyptians either. He had tried to make things better in his own strength without God's guidance and failed. So he fled from Pharaoh's presence and went into Midian, an area beyond the Red Sea in the Arabian Peninsula. Ironically, after such a privileged upbringing, he could now only find safety in the emptiness of the desert. But events were about to unfold. Sitting at a well when the seven daughters of the priest of Midian came to fetch water, Moses rescued them from being bullied by some shepherds. As a result of this, he was brought to their home, where he stayed and married one of the daughters, Zipporah. The couple had a son whom Moses called Gershom, a name that implied he still felt an alien in a foreign land, as he did not feel the desert was his home. Years passed and the Pharaoh who knew Moses died. (See Exodus 1—2.)

And then one day something happened that would change Moses's life forever. Alone in the wilderness, he was going about his normal business of caring for his father-in-law Jethro's sheep, when he came to Horeb, a place of apparent emptiness yet described as the 'Mountain of God'. Moses's mind was alert, as he was keeping watch over his sheep. Suddenly he noticed a bush ablaze. Normally this would evoke only a little curiosity and perhaps a wondering, 'who set this bush alight?' But this bush was different. It burnt without being consumed. As Moses went over to investigate, he was confronted by a mystery (Exodus 3.3), which is described as 'the angel of the LORD'. What he experienced may be understood as an icon of God, a way into a deeper awareness of God, which was revealed not to Moses's physical eyes but to the eyes of his heart. This awesome presence was powerful and dangerous; fearful yet full of promise. Moses's divine encounter would be a turning point not only for him but for the Hebrew people, as we shall shortly see.

It is important to note that Moses is discovered by God rather than the other way round. In turning aside from his sheep tending, Moses shows his openness, and through this God is made known to him. Out of the bush, God calls, 'Moses, Moses!' The repetition of the name communicates the importance and urgency of the call, but also its personal nature: God knows Moses and calls him by his name. Moses gives his full attention and says, 'Here I am' (Genesis 22.1, 11). The holy one seeks us out for obedience in service, which brings perfect freedom. The question is far more about willingness than capability, as Moses is about to learn.

He is warned, 'Come no closer! Remove the sandals from your feet, for the place on which you are standing is holy ground.' The removal of sandals is an ancient act of reverence when coming before the divine presence, and is still practised in Islam and other religions. It is also a symbol of homecoming. Moses, who has felt an alien in a foreign land, is finding his true home with God. He will be asked to lead his people into freedom in the Promised Land, where they too will find their home in God. A patch of scrubland in the wilderness is transfigured: God is there in the seeming emptiness, waiting to be known. When we experience desert times, we can know that God will not leave us forever in the wilderness. Emptiness on its own is dangerous to our being, for it may lead to us being haunted by our own demons. Yet the desert can also blossom and reveal the presence and glory of God.

The desert is a great place for vision. Too often we are so preoccupied that God cannot enter our lives or our hearts: it's as if we are saying 'there is no room in this establishment for I am too busy'. We need to make space for the one who comes. Though we often see ourselves as seekers, we need to become aware that God is seeking us out. He comes to us, revealing himself to us through his world, through encounters with others, as well as in our own being.

The holy one continues, 'I am the God of your father, the God of Abraham, the God of Isaac, and the God of Jacob.' God is the covenant-making God, who has given promises to his people. At this point Moses hides his face, for he is afraid to look at God (Exodus 3.5–6). If we do not sense our own unworthiness and lack of ability, if we do not feel fear and tremble at the presence and great otherness of God, then it is possible we have not yet experienced the living God but only ideas of him.

God reveals himself as a God who cares, a God of compassion. He is concerned with the poor and the oppressed; he seeks to help those who have no helper. God says, 'I have observed . . . I have heard their cry . . . I know their sufferings . . . I have come down to deliver them . . . and to bring them up out of that land' (Exodus 3.7–9). It all sounds too wonderful and awesome to be true! Then comes the punchline, which earths our loving God's promises. He says to Moses: 'I will send you to Pharaoh to bring my people, the Israelites, out of Egypt' (Exodus 3.10). The great truth is that our God is a God who sends us to work for his purpose for the world. He calls us to share in his compassion, and if we fail to do so, we betray any vision of God we may have seen, for vision demands response to its insights. To be hostile to another person or to ignore that person's need is to betray what we say with our lips about the God of love. The compassionate one asks us to respond with compassion: the God of love wants us to reveal his love. The God who comes down to rescue us demands that we take this to heart. One of my favourite descriptions of a priest is 'someone who has come down in the world'. We have to be found where the need is and not forever be protecting ourselves and trying to avoid seeing where we might help.

We may sometimes delude ourselves into thinking we have a high position in society, or that we can easily cope with what lies before us. This is not a trap Moses falls into here! He objects to God that he has already fled from the court of Pharaoh, and anyway, how can God expect him, a nomadic shepherd, to pit his puny might against the power of the great Egyptian Empire? In his last unfortunate encounter with the Hebrews, even his own people did not accept him. He appreciates that God needs someone as a representative, but he queries this, saying, 'Who am I that I should go to Pharaoh?' (Exodus 3.11). To the now fearful Moses God makes the greatest promise of all: 'I will be with you' (Exodus 3.12, cf. Isaiah 43.1–3). Through his living relationship with the Almighty God, Moses will be empowered from on high to fulfil his task, for God will work with him, through him and for him. God has turned Moses away from fretting about his own lack of ability and changed his focus to the power of the Almighty. He will not be alone in his task, for the Lord is at hand. Moses will prove the truth in the saying of John Knox the Scottish Reformer (1505–72): 'A man with God is always a majority.'

God often chooses the weak and the foolish that through them his strength may be revealed (1 Corinthians 1.26–29). What God asks for is our obedience, our willingness to go where he desires. We are not called because we are fully equipped for the task: it is our readiness that is important. The Church today has great resources for it is made up of countless gifted human beings, but we so often fail to achieve what we might do for God through lack of volition. It is our unwillingness to react to his call that so often hinders God's work. God will continue to challenge us with a vision of what could be if we work to reveal his saving power and love. This vision asks for a response in the same way that love needs a response. As God has given and continues to give himself to us, will we learn to give ourselves fully to him? It is only when we enter into this two-way relationship that we can experience the new freedom and power it brings – what St Paul calls the 'glorious liberty of the children of God'.

Moses, dazed by what he is experiencing, asks God, 'What shall I tell them about you, whom shall I say that you are, what is your nature and name?' You can imagine that it will be difficult for Moses to explain that God has called to him from a burning bush and reassured him that he has heard his people's cries for help. God replies by linking his name with the verb 'to be'. God says '*ehyeh asher ehyeh*', which is usually translated, 'I AM WHO I AM' (Exodus 3.14). We might read in this a mild rebuke to Moses's question, or an invitation to 'Search me out and know me'. Many prefer the translation to be put into the future tense, 'I will be what I will be.' But no words or tense can do justice to the nature of God, what God is or what he will be. He is the God who was with Abraham, Isaac and Jacob. He is the God who is with Moses and his people now, and the God who will go ahead of them, leading the way to the Promised Land.

We need never fear that God is a figment of our imagination: he is the living God, the eternal one, who is revealed in what he has done, what he is and what he will be. The wholly other comes to us and is among us. He can be discovered through a personal, living relationship, which can never be fully explained but may be described by the word 'faith'. Only those who have had some encounter with him can understand what we mean when we talk of our awesome God. For Moses, the God of his fathers, the God of history, the God of past experience, the God who was, has become the living God, whom he now personally encounters. The great 'I am' is hardly someone he can relegate to the past! This experience of Moses is something we all need to undergo. God may be beyond explanation and comprehension, but he is not beyond our apprehension.

God's 'I am what I am' reminds us that he is not restricted by his attributes or by the way we recognize him. He is more than the sum total of all our experiences. He is both the God who is the same yesterday, today and forever, and the dynamic God we can perceive actively involved in the newness of each day and each event. He makes all things new and may be met in multitudinous ways. Our whole existence is within this great other; nothing is outside him or beyond him. Yet we may spend our lives seeking the one who is already present, or running away from him who seeks us out. It is a wonderful moment when God is able to enter our life and say 'I am', and we discover he is not a theory but a personal God, seeking a personal relationship.

There will always be a temptation to enclose God within the framework of our understanding, where we can explain him and name him. This indicates a desire to control, but God can no more be captured than we could capture the essence of a living flower by pressing it and keeping it between the pages of a book. No individual being can ever be fully caught; though we do our best to describe someone in words, we can never quite convey that person's unique mystery and otherness. If this is true of human beings, how much more must it be true of God? We slowly learn that God is greater than all our thoughts and that the mind alone cannot contain him. The early Celtic people of the British Isles refused to try to write down any of the great mysteries, for they believed they could not be contained in a book, but only in the heart. The Zen Buddhists have a saying that fits this well: 'he who speaks does not know, he who knows does not speak.' Yet we do have to try and tell of God's presence and of his love.

Perhaps the emptiness of the desert was a crucial element in Moses's encounter with God. Though God took the initiative and called Moses, God did need Moses's human response. Moses would have to come to a decision, and after God promised that he would be with him from now on, we can have no doubt that Moses was aflame for God, ready to do wonders in God's power. In the same way after Pentecost, God empowered the very ordinary men who were the disciples to go out into the world.

If Moses had not been ready to turn aside from his humdrum activities, he would not have experienced the burning bush. Sadly, many people find life dull, ordinary and often empty, but there are those who live in awe, who find life and the world around them extraordinary and full of wonder. The burning bush was a visible sign not only of the presence but the power and purpose of God. Elizabeth Barrett Browning communicates this vividly in one of my favourite poems, *Aurora Leigh*:

> . . . Earth's crammed with heaven,
> And every common bush afire with God:
> But only he who sees, takes off his shoes;
> The rest sit around it, and pluck the blackberries,
> And daub their natural faces, unaware
> More and more, from the first similitude.[2]

Seeing is more than looking with only the eyes; it is a meeting with the other. To encounter creation is to discover that it is full of mystery and ready to reveal its wonders to us. It's a matter of learning to see everything as a subject in its own right, ready and able to communicate to us, if we simply open ourselves to what it has to say. The offering of our

65

undivided attention to anything is an act of love, of self-giving. 'Things' do not separate us from God: they are not his rivals but rather can awaken us, make us more alert, aware. To discover the extra-ordinariness of things, to enter into life's depths, is to discover worlds within worlds, wonder upon wonder.

The great wonder Moses saw caused him to turn not only from watching sheep but back towards Egypt. Perhaps we have allowed our lives to become too full and our minds too occupied for God to be able to speak to us. Yet our lives will be transformed by the revealing of the holy one. The ground on which we are standing is holy ground, for when we have found one truly holy place, all places become holy. We need to be able to say with Jacob, 'Surely the Lord is in this place and I knew it not.' Be open enough, be empty enough, to let God find you.

I often think upon these words of Teilhard de Chardin:

> God is not far away from us, altogether apart from the world we see, touch, hear, smell and taste about us. Rather he awaits us at every instant of our action.[3]

Exercises

1 Pray

Lord God, Holy and Almighty One,
Draw me aside to be aware of you.
Let the flame of your presence burn within my heart
And set me on fire with love for you:
On fire with love for your world
On fire with love for all people.

May my life radiate the warmth of your love,
Lord God, Holy and Almighty One.

2 The 5p exercise

Pause Turn aside from what is occupying you now and seek to be open to God for a little time this day. Breathe gently and deeply, making sure you are comfortable and that each part of your body is relaxed. Think of a restful scene and give your attention to it. Leave behind the troubles and the agendas of today and be at peace. After a while seek to become aware of what is around you.

Presence The God whom you seek is with you and seeking you in love. Remind yourself, 'I am loved by God.' The very place where you are at this moment is holy ground, for the Lord is with you. Speak to God and affirm his presence. You may like to say, 'God you are here: you are with me.' Say it with meaning. You may like to shorten the phrase and simply say 'God you are.' You can reduce the words once more and simply say, with love and adoration, 'God.' If you feel the need, repeat this affirmation more than once.

Picture Read Exodus 3.1–15. Visualize the scene. Though we're in the wilderness, there will be some spare pasture and scrub bushes. Moses has his sheep nearby. How would you see the burning bush? Analysis is less relevant here than wonder and awe. See Moses turning aside and giving it his attention. What reactions are appropriate – puzzlement, fear, worship? Now the voice that calls his name warns him to come no closer. Watch as Moses takes off his shoes and bows in adoration. God is saying he will send him to Pharaoh: see

Moses's reaction changing to fear as he asks, 'Who, me?' But God has empowered him and promises to go with him. This will make a great difference, yet Moses will still have some natural human doubts about his own ability. He will be able to perform his great task because of his willingness to cooperate and work out what God wants of him.

Ponder Have you learnt to turn aside, to give God some time and space in your life? Or have you allowed your agenda to be so full that this seems scarcely possible? Have you found a holy place that you can return to?

God calls you as you are. Think of your calling. What does God require of you? God does not leave you. How can your life reflect his presence?

Promise that you will make a space in your daily routine to allow God to find entrance; that you will seek to see what the loving compassionate God requires of you.

3 Final prayer

To you we come, God, our Creator,
Strength in our weakness:
Light in our darkness:
Peace in our distress:
Presence with us always:
Support us when our hearts are heavy.
Comfort us when we feel alone.
Refresh us when life feels like a desert.
Be a home to us when we are as aliens in a foreign land.
Lord as you abide with us, let us abide in you.
To you we come, God, our Creator.

6

❧ Strength in our weakness ❧

No worst, there is none. Pitched past pitch of grief,
More pangs will, schooled at forepangs, wilder wring.
Comforter, where, where is your comforting?
. . .
O the mind, mind has mountains; cliffs of fall
Frightful, sheer, no-man-fathomed. Hold them cheap
May who ne'er hung there. Nor does long our small
Durance deal with that steep or deep. Here! creep
Wretch, under a comfort serves as a whirlwind: all
Life death does end and each day dies with sleep.[1]

Gerard Manley Hopkins writes from experience, knowing only
too well the 'cliffs of fall'. Between 1877 and 1881 he worked
in London, Oxford, Liverpool, Glasgow and Chesterfield as
a Roman Catholic parish priest, and was deeply oppressed
by the poverty he witnessed. Hopkins longed for what he
called a 'working strength' to help 'dear and dogged man'.
But he often felt down, and the nervous disabilities that
affected him contributed to his exhaustion and the need for
rest. When he wrote of the dreaded 'cliffs of fall', he realized
only those who had suffered in a similar way would be able
to comprehend his meaning. As a parallel, we might think
of soldiers returning from the First World War telling family
and friends that unless they'd been there, they couldn't begin

to understand. But the 'cliffs of fall' are not wholly negative. If you have ever looked down from a mountain ridge, or from the great height of a precipice to rocks below, you will remember feeling both exhilaration and fear. Such an experience often triggers the realization that the higher we ascend, the further there is to fall. But to avoid the peak out of fear means we deprive ourselves of the joy of gaining the summit.

Similarly, to open our life to glory is to open it also to grief. In any great achievement there is the potential for disintegration, for a crash. Though we seek light and joy, we are bound to discover darkness and desolation along the way. Of course, you can try to live safely and avoid intense emotions like joy and despair, but a human being *fully alive* will experience everything. I find these words on vision inspire me:

> What is necessary first for visionary power is an undaunted appetite for liveliness – to be among the active elements of the world and love what they do to you, to love 'to work and to be wrought upon'; to be 'alive to all that is enjoyed and all that is endured', to have the loneliness and the courage to take in not only joy but dismay and fear and pain as modes of being without bolting for comfort or obscuring them with social chatter.[2]

Anyone who is living to the full will discover that there are days when they simply run out of resources. My parents would tell me, in an encouraging kind of way, when I was stretching my abilities, 'You never know your limits until you have exceeded them!' Our personal resources – and those of our planet – are restricted, and if we go beyond them, we will run into trouble. I've met many people who have suffered from complete burnout, who have been unable to do anything until they have been refreshed and renewed.

We will all experience moments when the journey of life feels too hard or too dark: there were times in the autumn of 2014 when many struggled to give proper attention to the news, such were the number of dreadful things that appeared to be happening on the world stage. And even on those days when, though the challenges facing us seem overwhelming, we are disciplined enough to get up out of bed and face the day, we may find that nothing goes to plan. To assume we are in control is one of the illusions of life and sooner or later that illusion is shattered. The able-bodied can suddenly feel burnt out, as if all power supply has been cut off. And like a car when its battery is flat, the more we try to 'rev' ourselves up, the worse things will get. We are not all-powerful, and the worst thing anyone can suggest to us when we're going through burnout or depression, is that we just need to pick ourselves up. That is an impossibility. All we can do is be still and wait for our resources to be restored, resting and relying on friends to be our strength and support. Christians at such times have the opportunity to learn to rest in God and give him the chance to renew us and revive us.

We can only love God because he first loved us, and though he is with us, we must be open to let him come to us. He often calls to us in the darkness and weakness of our lives, as the prophet Isaiah reminds us:

> The LORD is the everlasting God, the Creator of the ends of the earth. He does not faint or grow weary; his

understanding is unsearchable. He gives power to the faint, and strengthens the powerless. Even youths will faint and be weary, and the young will fall exhausted; but those who wait for the LORD shall renew their strength, they shall mount up with wings like eagles, they shall run and not be weary, they shall walk and not faint.   (Isaiah 40.28–31)

The story of Elijah reveals a man full of life and power. Elijah stands twice against King Ahab of Israel (1 Kings 17.1 and 18.17–18); after being fed by the widow of Zarephath, he performs a miracle with the supplying of provisions; and when the son of the widow dies, through God's power Elijah brings him back to life (1 Kings 17.8–24). Not long after, we hear of his single-handed triumph over 450 prophets of Baal on Mount Carmel, which is one of the most dramatic accounts in the Old Testament. Elijah has the people shouting, 'The LORD indeed is God; the LORD indeed is God' (1 Kings 18.17–39). There is no doubt he is a great prophet, and a mighty man of God. However, after Mount Carmel, Elijah spends more energy having the 450 prophets of Baal exterminated (1 Kings 18.40) – which is one way to get rid of the opposition! But this was not what God asked him to do, and it costs him dearly. Without God's aid Elijah runs out of power: alone, his resources limited.

1 Kings 19 comes as a shock after the stirring events of the previous two chapters. The invincible becomes vulnerable, the defeater is defeated. The powerful Elijah who stood against King Ahab and 450 prophets runs from one woman! Ahab's queen, Jezebel, the protector and patron of the prophets of Baal, is furious with Elijah. She sends a threatening

message saying she will have his life for what he has done. The mighty man, drained, fearful and discouraged, simply flees. He goes to Beersheba, the southernmost part of the kingdom of Judah, beyond the boundaries of Jezebel's northern kingdom. There Elijah leaves his manservant and sets off on a day's walk into the desert. Taking nothing with him, he cannot hope to last long. Is this a suicide attempt or a desire to force God's hand? God has provided food twice before in times of crisis: Elijah was fed by the ravens when he hid by the Wadi Cherith (1 Kings 17.1–7), and nourished by the poor widow when there was a famine in the land (1 Kings 17.8–16). Whatever his motivation, he lies down under a bush and asks to die. He just cannot go on. He has failed in encouraging Israel to worship the one God; he has lost any awareness of God's power in his life; he feels his life is over.

But God is not finished with Elijah. Even when Elijah has given up on himself, God's concern for him remains. An angel comes, awakens him and offers him food and drink, the two essentials for survival in the desert. There is no reason why this messenger of God may not have been an ordinary caring person. The angelic and the human are not incompatible, and when I am asked which this messenger might be, I always want to answer; I believe he could be both. When God sends a messenger to do his work, that envoy can rightly be described as an 'angel'. Elijah takes the refreshment he is offered but then falls asleep again, showing he has not yet recovered from his exhaustion. The angel rouses Elijah a second time and urges him to eat and drink, now providing a reason, 'otherwise the journey will be too much for you' (1 Kings 19.1–8). Elijah cannot go in his own strength; he needs the power provided by God through his angel.

After his second sleep, verse 8 indicates that Elijah's vitality is beginning to return. He rises, eats, drinks and goes out in the strength he has been given: there is no sign of a death wish now! After travelling 40 days and nights, he reaches Horeb and rests the night in a cave (1 Kings 19.9). On a practical level this journey seems to make little sense: Elijah is just recovering from lack of vision and energy, so why such an awesome journey through the desert? We need to remember that this is the desert where Moses saw the burning bush (Exodus 3.1). Horeb is the mountain of God, associated with God's appearances to Moses: it is also associated with covenant-making and God's giving of the law. It would appear Elijah is seeking to walk in the footsteps of Moses, to make a personal pilgrimage. The 40-day journey is to reflect the 40 years Moses spent in the wilderness, where he too was provided with 'heavenly food' (Exodus 16.35). Forty was also the number of days Moses spent on this mountain, and tradition suggests that Elijah went into the cave where Moses saw God's glory passing by (see Exodus 33.21–23). It would appear that Elijah is not only pushing himself but also seeking to push God into granting him the experience Moses had on this spot. But whatever happens will happen through God's grace alone. We cannot manoeuvre God through our actions, though we can seek out a holy place, somewhere God has been known to act, and stay there a while, waiting openly upon God. This is all Elijah can do.

And the Lord speaks to Elijah, saying, 'What are you doing here, Elijah?' As we've already seen, often in life we find ourselves asking, 'Where is God?', when all the time God is seeking an entrance into our life, saying to us, 'Where are you?' We go looking for the one who is waiting for us to be open to his presence. Elijah is on a spiritual journey – as all life should be – not simply on a trek through the desert. Already, through God's grace, he has been restored to physical well-being by the provision of life-giving food and drink. Now on Horeb, he seeks new vision and strength of spirit.

Yet the question from God appears to contain a reproach. God's prophets are not meant to be hiding away in caves: they should be out in the world, delivering divine messages in the very thick of life. Elijah's reply reveals that he is still sorry for himself and feeling alone and oppressed. He believes he is the only one doing God's work, yet we have been told that Obadiah, who is in charge of the palace, has hidden from Jezebel 100 of the prophets of the Lord in two caves, and is providing them with bread and water (1 Kings 18.3–4). Elijah is still taking far too much on his own shoulders. God says to him, 'Go out and stand on the mountain before the LORD, for the LORD is about to pass by' (1 Kings 19.11). This is an invitation to awareness: God is always 'passing by' to those with open eyes and hearts. In the Gospel of Luke the blind man became aware and 'saw' that someone important was passing by. In seeking to find out who, and then calling upon Jesus, he was healed (Luke 18.35–43). Perhaps you need to pray, 'Lord, may I receive my sight.' Life's pilgrimage should always be a journey into a deeper awareness of God.

As Elijah stands outside the cave there comes a great wind, but the Lord is not in the wind. This is followed by an earthquake, but the Lord is not in the earthquake. Then comes a fire, but the Lord is not in the fire. The three physical events that Moses experienced on the mountain (Exodus 19.16–18) are repeated here. However, disturbing signs in the weather and the world may be less indicative of God's presence than they are reflections of our own inner turmoil. We do not see what truly is but rather as it seems through our own limited vision. We cannot make God appear simply by seeking wind or earthquake or fire. Such signs are only pointers, and although they may direct us, they are not the presence themselves. True indications of the beyond in our midst lead us to the indescribable, which is outside our comprehension though not our apprehension. We can never know or understand God fully by our minds alone, but we can know him in our heart and being.

Elijah did not find God in earthquake, wind or fire. It was as if he were seeking to make God act by imitating Moses and it just didn't work. God wants us to be ourselves, not a copy of someone else. We cannot automatically conjure up an awareness of his presence through doing what someone else has done – we can only wait in openness before him. Consider the counsel given to the children at the end of *The Lion, the Witch and the Wardrobe*:

I don't think it would be any good trying to get back through the wardrobe door to get the coats. You won't get to Narnia again by *that* route . . . Yes, of course you'll get back to Narnia again some day . . . But don't go trying to use the same route twice. Indeed, don't *try* to get there at all. It'll happen when you are not looking for it. And don't talk too much about it even among yourselves. And don't mention it to anyone unless you find that they've had adventures of the same sort ... Keep your eyes open.[3]

This is great advice about not trying too hard – in fact about not trying, full stop! Sometimes our very prayers are so busy they prevent us being aware that God is seeking to speak to us. We do not get to know him because we are too busy talking; we do not realize he is beside us because we are too actively searching for him. The guidance of the Professor is 'don't talk too much – Keep your eyes open.' Similar advice comes in the Psalms, 'Be still, and know that I am God!' (Psalm 46.10). In the quieting of our activity, we make space in our lives for the Lord to enter and be known.

Elijah now stands in the stillness after the storm and waits upon God. In the sheer silence comes a voice asking the same question as before, 'What are you doing here, Elijah?' Repeating the question suggests that God is not pleased with Elijah's actions, while the prophet's reply shows that he still feels the burden of his task is too much. He is full of his own importance and all too ready to justify himself. God does not respond directly to Elijah's desires, but directs him to return by the route he came: 'Go on your way.' Elijah is to retrace his steps across the wilderness to Damascus and to anoint Hazael as king over Aram. He is then to anoint Jehu as king of Israel and Elisha as his own prophetic successor. God's words are intended to empower the prophet to return to where God has a purpose for him. He is back in God's service, but God tells him he is not the only one at work. There is still a substantial community who keep faith with God: 7,000 Israelites have not bowed to Baal, so Elijah need not be so discouraged or take himself so seriously because he is far from being the only person committed to the divine cause. After this time with God, Elijah is refreshed and renewed and returns to his work.

One word we come across again and again when God grants a vision is 'Go'. Vision is rarely for our delight alone but usually acts as a directive, giving a sense of purpose and meaning to what we are seeking to do. Spending time in contemplation and prayer is certainly good but these should normally result in action.

Sadly, I have met many ministers who have lost their high sense of calling and become pessimistic about the abilities of their congregation, while developing an exaggerated idea of their own importance. A similar attitude can be found in many secular leaders who have inflated ideas of themselves and their power. Elijah has rather fallen into this trap: he begins his response to God by telling of his own efforts, and comparing his zeal with the unfaithfulness of the Israelites. He gives the impression that everything hinges on him, claiming he is the only remaining prophet of the Lord, and that now even his life is endangered. It is as if God depends on him rather than the other way around. Given our limited resources, we all need to learn to lean on God for our strength and abilities, and for their renewal. We will discover that even when we lose our grip on God, God still keeps his hold of us. Though we may desert him – or find that everyone seems to be deserting us – God remains with us and will never leave us. When we have failed in our trust of God, he will still be faithful to us. At times of grief, of darkness, of entering the desert of despair and experiencing the cliffs of fall, God is there – and underneath are the everlasting arms.

Exercises

1 Pray

This prayer from the Outer Hebrides expresses the presence of God in our lives. Even when we do not feel that presence, we can still affirm it. I suggest this is a prayer worth learning by heart and using regularly.

> **God's Aid**
> God to enfold me,
> God to surround me,
> God in my speaking,
> God in my thinking.
>
> God in my sleeping,
> God in my waking,
> God in my watching,
> God in my hoping.
>
> God in my life,
> God in my lips,
> God in my soul,
> God in my heart.
>
> God in my sufficing,
> God in my slumber,
> God in mine ever-living soul,
> God in mine eternity.[4]

2 The 5p exercise

Pause It is important to stop the whirlwind of your activities; to still the tempest of your thoughts, and to get away for a while from all earth-shattering events. You are not all-mighty and you need to be recharged and refreshed. Be still and allow God space to be a presence in your life. Seek to relax. Do not do anything except make sure you are comfortable and not tense. Be still. It will take practice but you can do it. Be still.

Presence Turn your whole being to wait upon God. You cannot imagine him but he is with you. The reason you are creating this space is for the love of God: his love for you and your love for him. Rest in his presence as you would in that of a loved one. There is no need for words. If your mind wanders, bring it back by affirming, 'Lord God you are with me.' If it continues to wander, bring it back again and affirm, 'Lord God you are.' After that, if it is still wandering, simply say with love, 'Lord God,' and seek to rest in him.

Picture Read 1 Kings 19.1–13. Elijah is a great prophet, filled with the power of God. He has just won a victory single-handed (do not forget God has been working in him) against hundreds of false prophets who were leading the people astray. He has withstood 450 men and now he is on the run from one woman. How like a man! True, she is a queen, and Jezebel is known to be fierce. Elijah is exhausted by his ordeal on Carmel. He is utterly drained. Having no energy to fight he flees to the desert, and there he desires to die. Yet in the emptiness he is visited and refreshed. Elijah's powers are being restored and he goes a long distance before sheltering in a cave. There in silence he hears God say, 'What are you doing here?' It is worth noticing that God is there in the cave, as he will be wherever his prophet goes. God wants Elijah to turn to him, to be aware of him. There is a great storm, an earthquake, wind and fire. Elijah wraps himself in his cloak and watches this display of power. Afterwards there is silence, stillness after the storm. In the stillness, Elijah hears God, is filled with God and is able to continue his work for God.

Ponder How often have you found yourself in a wilderness, out of resources and unable to go on? Have you understood this as some sort of message or have you just run for refuge?

Emptiness is always capable of being filled by God. The desert in our lives, as well as the actual desert, is where God is often found and where God is seeking to speak to us. Because God will not force himself upon us, it is necessary for us to find a space to let him in – or to discover in ourselves the space that is made for him alone.

Do you recognize feelings of emptiness and of boredom as cries to be filled with God?

Are your prayers full of instructions telling God what you want? Or do you try to wait upon God to see what he wants of you?

How much space do you make in your life for God to speak to you?

Perhaps you can find ways of being more open to God: letting him 'find' you rather than forever seeking him.

Promise to make room each day for God to come and speak to you. Without a fixed time and place there is a danger that you will not meet God anywhere or at any time, so choose your time and place and then rest in God's presence. You will find it is soon possible to meet God everywhere and at any moment of the day.

Do not let activity crowd out your quiet time with God.

3 Final prayer

I weave a silence on to my lips
I weave a silence into my mind
I weave a silence into my heart
I close my ears to distractions
I close my eyes to attractions
I close my heart to temptations.

Calm me, O Lord, as you stilled the storm
Still me, O Lord, keep me from harm
Let all the tumult within me cease
Enfold me Lord in your peace.[5]

7

꒰ *The shaking of the foundations* ꒱

> O world invisible, we view thee,
> O world intangible, we touch thee,
> O world unknowable, we know thee,
> Inapprehensible, we clutch thee!
>
> Does the fish soar to find the ocean,
> The eagle plunge to find the air –
> That we ask of the stars in motion
> If they have rumour of thee there?[1]

There are occasions in our lives when we are brought up with a start. Something happens – whether a sudden accident, a serious illness, the death of a loved one, or being made redundant at work – which makes it feel as if our very foundations have been shaken and our whole world is falling apart. The prophet Isaiah underwent such an experience. It caused him to despair, but then he opened his eyes to a greater world where God is present and in control.

Isaiah gives us the exact date of his vision: it was the year that King Uzziah died, 740–739 BC (Isaiah 6.1). Uzziah began his 52-year reign when he was only 16 years old. The nation of Judah must have wondered how they would fare under such a young monarch, yet he proved a good ruler in many ways: 'he did what was right in the sight of

the LORD' (2 Chronicles 26.4). Over half a century, he brought
stability and prosperity to the nation. A strong man with
a large army, he was successful in his battles against the
Philistines and Arabs. He reinforced the walls of Jerusalem
and provided new weapons for their defence. He had shepherds, farmers and vine-dressers working for him, and
was described as someone who loved the soil (2 Chronicles
26.10). Out in the countryside, he had fortified towers
and cisterns built to provide water. It was under this
God-fearing king, and during this period of security, that
Isaiah began his life's work. Yet Uzziah had his faults. Late
in life, he proudly entered the area of the Temple where
only priests were allowed to offer incense. During the confrontation with 80 priests that followed, the raging king's
face was seen to become leprous. From that day until he
died, Uzziah's leprosy forced him to live separately. He
could no longer fulfil his duties as king and his son acted
as regent.

For Isaiah this was disastrous. The king he was used to
working under was no longer able to function. No doubt
Isaiah prayed for the king's recovery, but he died and the
throne became empty. How would the nation fare? How
would he fare? Who would take control now? Isaiah went
into the Temple with his mind racing. And then it happened.
He perceived in a vision that the throne was not empty, for
'I saw the Lord sitting on a throne, high and lofty; and the
hem of his robe filled the Temple' (Isaiah 6.1). In the midst
of Isaiah's emptiness – which echoed that of the throne – it
was revealed that the true king of all the earth is the Lord.
Often we need some kind of loss or shock to realize that our
God is still with us. Isaiah said 'I saw the Lord' – though no

one can see God in his fullness and live (Exodus 33.20) – and was aware of the presence of God, the God who is in control, filling the Temple. This encounter would mark Isaiah's whole ministry, for it was at this moment that the truth dawned that God is not far off; rather God is with us and God is in control. He is not a theory enclosed in sacred books or locked away in the holy of holies, but a living and present God with whom we have to do.

Isaiah's vision continued; he saw the angelic attendants of God, who correspond in many ways to the golden cherubim covering the Ark of the Covenant in the holy of holies. Isaiah heard them calling to each other, 'Holy, holy, holy is the LORD of hosts' (Isaiah 6.3). Not once only but three times God was declared as holy. The Hebrew people used repetition to communicate intensity. Describing the Lord as holy is very special, and to repeat this three times is to affirm holiness in the highest possible degree. The holy of holies is not the possession of a priestly caste but exists in all the world. Holy means 'set apart', either for a purpose or because something is totally different. God is not like any creature and his being is beyond our complete understanding. If this were all we could say, we might decide we could never know God, for our minds simply cannot grasp what God is really like. However, as God revealed himself to Isaiah, so he reveals himself in many ways to us.

For Isaiah the veil of the Temple seemed to be open and he could see into the holy of holies, the place of God's hidden glory where only the high priest was allowed to go once a year; Isaiah saw beyond the physical place into the very presence of God. That presence filled the whole Temple, but Isaiah perceived that this glory of God is not hidden away from humankind, for the seraphim declared 'the whole earth is full of His glory'. Though God is beyond our comprehension he is not separate from us. Indeed, Isaiah would expand this to declare 'God is with us' in the naming of Emmanuel (Isaiah 7.14). Glory is a manifestation of the presence of God, and though hidden from our sight, it may be perceived by those with eyes to see, ears to hear and hearts that love. Heaven and earth are full of God's glory, his hidden presence, and we can apprehend it, though never fully comprehend it.

I can still remember being asked to write an essay on 'glory'. I already knew that the Hebrew word for glory was *Shekinah* and the Greek word was *doxa*. Both described a hidden presence. The imagery for that hidden presence was the veil of the Temple, or a cloud with the sun hidden behind it, as often depicted in art and stained glass windows. But I needed more, so I turned to a theological work. The words were laid out alphabetically and it was easy to look up glory, but all the entry said was 'see God'! I closed the book firmly, for I knew the answer without seeking further. Glory comes with our being aware of God. As I struggled to compose the essay, I felt like Hilary of Poitiers writing *On the Trinity* when he said:

We are compelled to attempt what is unattainable, to climb where we cannot reach, to speak what we cannot utter; instead of the mere adoration of faith, we are compelled to entrust the deep things of religion to the perils of human experience.

I would have preferred to write very little and to reflect on the hymn 'Bright the vision that delighted' by Richard Mant (1776–1848), especially the verse:

Lord, thy glory fills the heaven;
Earth is with its fullness stored;
Unto thee be glory given,
Holy, holy, holy, Lord.

This hymn of praise seeks to capture the vision of Isaiah and affirms the glory of God's presence to be found in our world. Psalm 19 declares the same in its first verse: 'The heavens are telling the glory of God; and the firmament proclaims his handiwork.' The glory of God should open our eyes and touch our hearts, and I have often reflected on this in my writing, from my first book, *The Edge of Glory*, through to *Glimpses of Glory*, *Clouds and Glory*, *Traces of Glory* and the omnibus, *Radiance of his Glory*. In another book, *Walking the Edges*, I wrote about how I believe that God and his glory wait to be revealed in all creation, including all people.

Within each piece of creation,
within each person,
the hidden God waits
to cause us to laugh and surprise us with
    his glory.

Within each moment of time,
within each day and each hour,
the hidden God approaches us
to call our name and to give us his joy.

Within each human heart,
within our innermost being,
the hidden God touches us
to awaken to his love and his presence.

> Everything is within Him,
> Space and time,
> The human being and the heart.
> God calls us to open our eyes
> and our hearts to Him and his will.[2]

The same God opens the eyes and the heart of Isaiah to his presence. But the presence of God is not necessarily a warm comfortable feeling; it can disturb and direct us. Isaiah's immediate reaction is one of awe, which makes him aware of his own unworthiness. 'Woe is me!' he declares, 'I am lost, for I am a man of unclean lips, and I live among a people of unclean lips; yet my eyes have seen the King, the LORD of hosts!' (Isaiah 6.5). Peter's reaction to the presence of Jesus in his boat is much the same: 'Go away from me, Lord, for I am a sinful man!' (Luke 5.8). Isaiah feels he will not survive having seen and heard the seraphim and having had a vision of the Lord of hosts. Like the rest of the people, he is unworthy, sinful and far from perfect. But our weaknesses do not give us an excuse to opt out. God does not seek perfection: he seeks those who are willing. He knows us and calls us though we have failed him. Once aware of his own unworthiness, Isaiah is open to the grace, goodness and guidance of God. God is a forgiving God (6.7).

Too often we feel that God keeps a balance sheet of our good and bad deeds and is ready to condemn us. Or that he only likes righteous people. But God does not condemn, and we condemn ourselves if we turn our backs on him and his love. He is always ready to accept those who turn to him and our unworthiness is of far less account than God's love and forgiveness. One of the most wonderful verses in the Scriptures is where Jesus says, 'anyone who comes to me I will never drive away' (John 6.37). This should make us all want to sing:

> Praise, my soul, the King of heaven,
> to his feet thy tribute bring;
> ransomed, healed, restored, forgiven,
> who like me his praise should sing?
> Alleluia, Alleluia, praise the everlasting King.[3]

When Isaiah sees the seraphim praising God and crying out 'Holy, holy, holy,' he realizes his own unworthiness. The seraphim are holy and he is not: they see God and live; his own awareness of God makes him feel he will die because 'no one can see God and live'. It is often necessary to appreciate how great God is and how we have failed him before we can move on. An experience of their own unworthiness is common among people who have had a vision of God.

'Then one of the seraphim flew to me, holding a live coal that had been taken from the altar with a pair of tongs' (Isaiah 6.6). The fire is from the altar, indicating that it is from the Lord. The seraph touches Isaiah's mouth with the burning coal, and says: 'Now that this has touched your lips, your guilt has departed and your sin is blotted out' (Isaiah 6.7). Only when Isaiah has 'seen' the Lord, been made aware of his sin and cleansed from its guilt, does the holy Lord speak to him directly: 'Then I heard the voice of the Lord saying, "Whom shall I send, and who will go for us?"' (Isaiah 6.8). God wants willing service – he will not force Isaiah any more than he would later have Mary be the mother of Jesus, unless she was prepared to undertake the role. God asks for freely given cooperation, because he wants to reach out to others through willing people.

Isaiah replies to God with the words, 'Here am I; send me!' (cf. Genesis 22.1ff., Luke 3.8). Isaiah is ready to serve God and to do his will. He has new courage, for he has been touched by the fire of God and God's grace is at work in his life. Hearing God's call, Isaiah responds, even though he does not know what he is responding to. Yet he is, genuinely, to be sent by God. Sometimes missions fail because people go out with versions of belief they are sure are right, but they have not been filled with God's power and loving presence. They may be offering their own idols rather than the living God. They may also give the impression that they own God and can dispense him to others.

Isaiah offers himself before he knows his task. Those who answer the call, God sends. Isaiah is not to work in the Temple but to go out among the people and give them the opportunity to turn to God. To tell them God is with them. Yet God warns Isaiah, 'the people will keep listening but not comprehend, keep looking but not understand'. The task will be neither an easy nor a rewarding one. It may be a privilege but it is also a great responsibility. Isaiah is to seek to bring people to a greater awareness of the holy God and of his glory in all the world. But by their reaction, they will show they are blind and deaf. The work of the Church is still to open the eyes of the blind, and to help the deaf to hear. Jesus told his disciples this was the difficulty of their task (Mark 4.10, cf. John 12.39–41, Acts 28.24–27, Romans 11.7–8). It sounds an impossible mission, but it would be less so if people made themselves available. God seeks to offer everyone the opportunity to turn to him and work with him. It is we who excuse and therefore exclude ourselves. God can only be fully active if our eyes, ears and hearts are opened. He can open the eyes of the blind, make the deaf hear and soften the hard-hearted, but only if we are willing to let him into our lives. We should regularly invite God to be at work in us: to heal our deafness and cure our blindness.

Isaiah now asks, 'How long, O Lord?' (Isaiah 6.11–13), which is a natural reaction from anyone who is given such a difficult commission. 'I have to preach to those who won't hear. How long will I have to serve in this way?' The reply is, as long as people are still there to listen, even in the midst of destruction, desolation and emptiness. Isaiah's task would be impossible without God's presence. Yet amidst the devastation, God's holy seed is there, waiting to grow, to restore, to renew (Isaiah 6.11–13). There is hope for the people for they are born of God (Isaiah 11.1). Though destruction and diminishment may be at hand, trust in God, for nothing can separate you from him and his love. This is a vision that many of us need once again in our lives. Whatever is happening, we are called to play our part.

Exercises

1 Pray

God, without whom nothing is strong, nothing is holy,
grant us a glimpse of your glory:
that our eyes may be opened
and the world transfigured for us;
that we may see your glory in all things,
and the entire earth full of your glory.

2 The 5p exercise

Pause Make a space in your life where God can be met and known. Keep a holy place somewhere but also in your heart. Come there and relax. Teach yourself to be still and quietly wait upon God. If your mind wanders, bring it back saying, 'Here I am, Lord,' and seek to be available to him. Then wait upon him in the stillness.

Presence Rejoice that you are not alone, for you are in the presence of the holy one, the loving and forgiving God. Rejoice that the whole world, including you, is already full of his glory. You may like to say:

> Lord, open my eyes to your presence.
> Lord, open my ears to your call.
> Lord, open my heart to your love.
> Lord, open my whole being to your glory.

Above all, seek to be open to God.

Picture Read Isaiah 6.1–8. Visualize a very distressed Isaiah in the Temple. No doubt Isaiah has been praying for the recovery of King Uzziah. But for all his petitions, Uzziah has got worse and died. The king has been Isaiah's patron, his security and his protection, and now the throne is empty. Under the king's care, Isaiah has flourished. He thought he had a future, but now he is very uncertain and the emptiness of the throne echoes the emptiness of his thoughts and his heart. He stands before it in despair. Then, suddenly, 'I saw the Lord sitting upon the throne.' Life and hope arise. Isaiah is not alone. The throne room becomes a holy place, for the Lord is here. The day and the world will change from this moment and Isaiah will change too, for nothing can be the same when God is in control. Try to express the difference it must make to be aware that 'the whole earth is full of his glory'.

Now see a fearful Isaiah, aware of his own unworthiness. He is a sinful person and he has seen the Lord. Reflect on the wonderful grace of God. He comes to us whether we are worthy or not: indeed, who is worthy? God comes to each of us and we need to open our eyes and our hearts to him. The test of our vision will be that it calls us to a higher level and a greater awareness of ourselves and others: vision requires action. Isaiah says: 'Here am I: send me!'

Ponder Do you seek to be open to God's glory or do you live as if the throne was empty and God had vacated his world?

We rarely turn to God in our daily tasks. Can you find ways of expressing his glory in your life?

Are you making the excuse of unworthiness for not seeking to work with God and for God?

Is it possible for you to find ways of offering your life to him?

Promise to make a space in each day to rejoice in God's presence, and to hear him speaking in the spaces in your life.

3 Think upon these words

Think upon these words by Teilhard de Chardin, and try to practise them:

> But once we have jealously safeguarded our relation to
> God, encountered, if I may dare use the expression, in

93

his 'pure state' (that is to say in a state of distinct being from all the constituents of the world), there is no need to fear that the most trivial or the most absorbing of occupations should force us to depart from him. To repeat: by virtue of creation and still more of the Incarnation, *nothing* here below is profane for those who know how to see. On the contrary everything is sacred . . . Try with God's help, to perceive the connection – even physical and natural – which binds your labour with the building of the kingdom of heaven.[4]

8

☙ *Coming home* ❧

God from whom to stray is to fall,
and to whom to return is to rise up,
in whom to remain is to rest on a firm foundation.
To leave you is to die,
to return to you is to come back to life,
to dwell in you is to live.
No one loses you if he does not fall into error,
no one seeks you without being called,
no one finds you without being purified.
To go away from you is to be lost,
to seek you is to love,
to see you is to make you our own.[1]

Apart from anything else, Jesus could be remembered as a really good storyteller. His parables, which have a simplicity and depth we are still exploring today, tell of the kingdom of God, and are crafted to challenge and change our way of thinking. Like the Bible as a whole, they are about encounters: they help us explore our relationships with ourselves, with others, with the world and with our God. If we hear the parables only as stories, it is likely that our ears and our hearts are not properly tuned in to what is being said. Jesus remarked that without insight and awareness of the kingdom of God, people might see him and hear him, but 'looking they may not perceive, and listening they may not understand' (Luke 8.10).

In chapter 15 of his Gospel, Luke gathers together a group of parables about seeking after the lost. The key to each story lies in the words of Jesus, 'I tell you, there will be more joy in heaven over one sinner who repents than over ninety-nine righteous people who need no repentance' (Luke 15.7, cf. 15.10 and 15.32). We read in the first account about a lost sheep, and we should be picturing not a sweet little lamb, but a wayward old ewe or ram that has wandered off into the wilderness. The shepherd will go after it until he finds it and will not give up (Luke 15.1–7). The second story tells of a woman who loses a silver coin and searches carefully until she finds it (Luke 15.8–10). This puts me in mind of a young nurse who once visited Holy Island on pilgrimage and lost a ring in the churchyard. When I first saw her, she was in tears. She had a bus to catch and the tide, which would cut Lindisfarne off from the mainland, was coming in fast. Yet she was insistent that she would not leave until she found the ring. I asked her if it was of great value and she replied, 'It would not be to you. It's not worth a lot, but it is precious to me and I'm going to seek for it until I find it.' She knew roughly where the ring should be but it was truly lost. I went home and returned with a metal detector, and in less than two minutes the ring was found. The young nurse thanked me, her face radiant with joy. We can be sure that we are no less precious, no less a source of delight, to the God who loves us and longs for us to return to him.

The parable usually known as 'The Prodigal Son' (Luke 15.11–32) could just as easily be called 'The Two Lost Brothers', for both are adrift in different ways. However I would like to call it 'The Loving Father', for it is really a story about how God loves us throughout our lives, even when we turn our back on him.

The parable may be divided into four scenes. In scene one, we find the younger son dissatisfied, wanting to leave home and to start a new life. He is keen to lay his hands on any material benefits he can to fund this, so he asks for his share of his father's property. To the Jews this would have sounded appalling: it is virtually saying to your father, 'I wish you were dead.' The unhappiness within the younger son spreads to his father, who is sorrowful that his son is leaving but will not hold him back. He could forbid him to go, but would rather the boy wanted to stay willingly, out of love. As the son gets what he wants then turns his back on his father and his home, he seems less than aware of the blessings he has already received, both in terms of the world he has grown up in and of the love lavished upon him. In his seeking to take but not to give in return, we see the separation that is caused when we try to become self-made men and women, refusing to recognize the grace and goodness of those who give to us, and believing we possess things in our own right. Entering the darkness of a self-centred life, it often will take us a long time to discover that 'without love we are nothing'.

Scene two shows the young man in a far country, squandering his father's gift in dissolute living. He may be having a great adventure, but it's not long before the money runs out. And as the land is hit by a severe famine, he begins to be in need. The emptiness he feels is all the more acute because there's no one around who cares for him. He is forced to hire himself out and – horror of horrors – he is sent to feed pigs. In Jewish thought, those dealing with pigs were contaminated, the lowest of the low. Things could hardly get worse for the young man, and indeed some would probably think he has got exactly what he deserves. But there among the pig swill, possibly at his lowest point, a faint light begins to dawn. The young man realizes how much better off he was before. He says to himself, 'I will arise and go to my father.' Entering into newness of life is a possibility for as long as we live, and in deciding to turn around, the younger son takes a decision to face his father and admit his own sinfulness and unworthiness. He will even offer himself as a hired hand. There is little doubt that we see a resurrection experience beginning to take place.

Throughout the Gospels, written of course after Christ rose from the dead, there are suggestions of resurrection, which have been 'lost in translation'. In the following places, the King James Version uses the word 'arise', while the New Revised Standard Version only has 'get up' or something similar.

In the story of the Prodigal Son (which we shall return to later on) we are told he said 'I will arise and go to my father' and that 'he arose' (Luke 15.18, 20, KJV).

Luke also tells the story of the only son of a widow at Nain. This young man has died and is being carried out for burial. Jesus, the Lord of life, stops the funeral procession, touches the bier and says to the young man, 'Arise' (Luke 7.14). He is restored and given back to his mother in newness of life.

In another story from Luke, Jesus is in the region between Samaria and Galilee when ten lepers approach him. Because of their infectious disease, lepers were not only banned from normal life; they were forbidden from making contact with

healthy people and already counted as dead. When one of
the ten returns to give thanks to Jesus for his healing and
prostrates himself at his feet, Jesus says, 'Arise, go thy way:
thy faith has made thee whole' (Luke 17.19) – truly an opportunity of new life.

Mark tells of a boy who apparently has some form of
epileptic fit. The boy falls down and is like a corpse before
Jesus. Most of those who are there say, 'He is dead. But Jesus
took him by the hand, and lifted him up; and he arose' (Mark
9.27, KJV).

Despite the wealth Matthew had amassed through collecting taxes, he was not much better off than the Prodigal Son.
Matthew was viewed as collaborating with the enemy, the
occupying Romans, and though of the priestly family of Levi,
his actions meant he was banned from worshipping with
his people. When he arose and followed Jesus, there is no
doubt that for Matthew resurrection was already at work
(Matthew 9.9). It may be no coincidence that the Gospel
places his calling by Jesus between two other 'resurrections':
the paralysed man who is commanded to arise in Matthew
9.5–6, and the dead girl who arises when Jesus takes her by
the hand in Matthew 9.25.

Time and again, each one of us is given the opportunity
to experience rising from what would keep us in captivity,
and to enter into the fullness of the glorious freedom of the
children of God. With St Patrick often I want to say:

> I arise today
> Through the mighty strength, the invocation
>   of the Trinity,
> Through belief in the threeness,

Through confession of the oneness
Of the Creator of Creation.

I arise today
Through the strength of Christ's birth with His
    baptism,
Through the strength of His crucifixion with His
    burial,
Through the strength of His resurrection with
    His ascension,
Through the strength of His descent for the
    judgement of doom.

I arise today . . .[2]

There is a sense in which we should allow every day to be a resurrection day: it would be a tragedy if we put the resurrection off to beyond the grave! Wonderful experiences will happen to us again and again, and it is good to recognize our mini-resurrections and to give thanks to God for each of them. At the start of some days, I like to use the words of John Keble's hymn that I mentioned earlier:

New every morning is the love
Our wakening and uprising prove;
Through sleep and darkness safely brought
Restored to life, and power, and thought.

New mercies each returning day,
Hover around us while we pray;
New perils past, new sins forgiven,
New thoughts of God, new hopes of heaven.[3]

In this sense I am trying to take to heart the words of Harry Williams in his book *True Resurrection*:

> If we have been aware of the resurrection in this life, then, and only then, shall we be able or ready to receive the hopes of final resurrection after physical death. Resurrection as our final and ultimate future can be known only by those who perceive resurrection with us now encompassing all we are and do. For only then will it be recognised as a country we have already entered and in whose light and warmth we have already lived. The possibility of the body's resurrection now in the present is thus of no mere theoretical interest. It is a matter of urgent concern.[4]

Seek to make every day of your life a resurrection day: a day when you turn again to the Father.

Let's return now to the Prodigal Son story and scene three. The son sets off, 'But while he was still far off, his father saw him and was filled with compassion; he ran and put his arms around him and kissed him' (Luke 15.20). Once again the Jews would have been reeling! Eastern men did not usually run because of their long clothing: it was thought quite unseemly. But the father runs to embrace and kiss the young man who has been wallowing with pigs. The son is ready to confess his unworthiness and to offer himself as a hired hand, but his father stops him before he can finish. Lovingly he is accepted, and with evident grace and forgiveness, clothed in the best robes. A ring is put on his finger and sandals on his feet. The rejoicing father says, 'let us eat and celebrate; for this son of mine was dead and is alive again; he was lost and is found!'

(Luke 15.24). Here is a declaration of resurrection, of one who is dead coming alive again; one who is lost being found.

Scene four sees the return of the elder son from working in the fields. He has heard the music and the dancing and has been wondering what is going on. When he is told everyone is celebrating the younger son's return, he refuses to go in. He is very angry with his brother but also with his father, declaring that he, his elder son, has slaved away for years and never disobeyed a command. Yet now he refuses his father's request to come into his home, and pointedly calls his brother 'this son of yours', wanting nothing to do with him. He reminds his father that his brother has wasted his inheritance on prostitutes. At this point in the story many of the Jewish listeners would have thought 'he's right, this wayward son did not deserve such a welcome'. But the father's response is to plead with the son to enter the house, and to remind him of his own possessions, saying, 'Son, you are always with me, and all that is mine is yours.' The father is reaching out to him in love.

Those listening to the parable with ears that were open would realize that many Jews were in a similar position to the elder son. God had offered them himself and all that he has, but they had counted this as just what they deserved, what they had earned through being law abiding. They still needed to discover the grace of God at work. Living by the law is not enough; we need to respond to the love of God. There is a sense in which at the end of the story – though we are not vouchsafed the final result – the elder son is not at home, for he refuses to come in and is not happy with what is happening there. But what is emphasized is that the father sees his sons as brothers: 'We had to celebrate and rejoice, because this brother of yours was dead and has come to life; he was lost and has been found' (Luke 15.32).

God's love for us never ceases, even when we turn our backs and wander away. He seeks us out, and makes it possible for us to rise to a new life and come home to him. God does not treat us like a possession, or demand that we submit to him: he does not punish us for our way-wardness but respects our freedom of choice. Our leaving him causes him sorrow and he longs for us to turn to him once more of our own free will. He wants us to see that living under the law, as the elder brother does, is not enough. We need to accept God's grace, forgiveness, accep-tance and love at work in our lives. What better way to end this scene than with these wonderful words from Julian of Norwich:

> I learned that love was our Lord's meaning.
> And I saw for certain, both here and elsewhere,
> that before ever he made us, God loved us;
> and that his love has never slackened,
> nor ever shall.
> In this love all his works have been done,
> and in this love he has made everything serve us;
> and in this love our life is everlasting.
> Our beginning was when we were made,
> but the love in which he made us never had a beginning.
> In it we have our beginning.
> All this we shall see in God forever.
> May Jesus grant this.[5]

Exercises

1 Give thanks

You may like to give thanks for God's love towards you using these words from the Psalms:

> Bless the LORD, O my soul, and all that is within me,
>   bless his holy name.
> Bless the LORD, O my soul, and do not forget all
>   his benefits –
> who forgives all your iniquity, who heals all your
>   diseases,
> who redeems your life from the Pit,
> who crowns you with steadfast love and mercy . . .
> The LORD is merciful and gracious,
> slow to anger and abounding in steadfast love . . .
> He will not always accuse, nor will he keep his
>   anger for ever.
> He does not deal with us according to our sins,
>   nor repay us according to our iniquities.
> For as the heavens are high above the earth, so great
>   is his steadfast love.

(Psalm 103.1–4, 8–11)

2 The 5p exercise

Pause Stop all that you are doing and be still. Allow the stillness to enter into your heart and mind. Rest in the love of God, seeking to be aware that when God offers you his love he offers you himself. There is no need for effort. Make sure your body is relaxed and your mind rested. Breathe in slowly and deeply. If the mind wants to wander, with each intake of breath affirm 'Lord, you love me', and as you exhale, affirm 'I abide in you'.

Presence Allow the love of God to enfold you. Immerse yourself in the love of God. Know that even when you lose your grip on God, he has you in his hands. As being aware of God and his love is of the utmost importance, spend a good part of this time rejoicing in his presence.

Picture Read the story of the Prodigal Son in Luke 15.11–32. Visualize the story as if it were a film. See the young son making his demands and causing so much unhappiness. The sale of one's inheritance is painful to anyone who has any sensitivity at all: it is robbing the future for immediate gratification. What use is it to gain things if you no longer feel at home in the world? Watch how the son turns his back on his father and sets off. The father stands watching with sadness but knows his son must venture. Though he could have made him stay, he wants the young man to have freedom of choice, to remain only of his own will, out of love.

Now see the son in a far country. Money buys him a lot of fun. He is having a great adventure. But his resources are limited. His supplies run out and famine comes. Now he is not much better off than an animal and he finds himself feeding with the pigs. What is worse, he is on his own and without love. His memories of good times surface and he realizes he is living well below par. He would be far better where he was loved. He decides to return. Is it at this point that his resurrection begins? He becomes aware of his unworthiness but also of his father's love. Picture him in this awareness.

Visualize the return. See how the father was waiting and responds to seeing his boy. He runs to meet him, hugs him, kisses him, clothes him, puts a ring on his finger, sandals on his feet and organizes a feast! He is accepted and cherished – a son who has returned from the dead and is being blessed with newness of life.

Now look at the other son, with a face like thunder. Surely there's more than a hint of jealousy here? He refuses to come in and talks of slavish obedience. How unaware of his father's love he seems to be. Does he not appreciate all the father has lavished on him? The elder son's anger keeps him outside. Yet the father goes out to him. Do you think this love was rejected?

Ponder Where do you fit into this story? Have you a sense of adventure? Are you willing to risk making mistakes? Or dare you not leave home?

Have you experienced the love of the Father for you, or do you feel more familiar with the idea of a God of vengeance?

Are there opportunities of resurrection, of turning and of newness of life that you can recall being offered to you?

Most of us have been both the Prodigal Son and the son who lived under law and failed to recognize love. We all need to discover the world of grace where God's love and God himself is not earned but freely given. Our actions can hurt love but the love of God is not destroyed. God welcomes you today. Have you learnt to turn to him and allow his love to enfold you? Can you experience in that love resurrection in your whole life?

Promise to seek and enjoy the presence of God each day. To be with God in your home and to live in the kingdom of God, which is always at hand.

3 Pray

Turn these wonderful words into a prayer of thanksgiving to the God of love:

> But this I call to mind, and therefore I have hope:
> the steadfast love of the LORD never ceases,
> his mercies never come to an end;
> they are new every morning;
> great is your faithfulness.
> 'The LORD is my portion,' says my soul,
> 'therefore I will hope in him.'
>
> (Lamentations 3.21–24)

9

✍ *Rejoicing in the Lord* ✍

Christ as a light
Illumine and guide me!
Christ as a shield overshadow and cover me!
Christ be under me! Christ be over me!
Christ be beside me,
On left hand and right!
Christ be before me, behind me, about me!
Christ, this day, be within and without me![1]

I was quite a timid child in some ways and didn't like a lot of outward show. Looking back many years now, I can clearly recall a moment in church which both terrified me and made a huge difference to my life, though I was slow to appreciate it at the time. Perhaps this was because I was only beginning to grow in awareness of God . . . I had gone to a choir practice in St Michael's Church, Alnwick, having recently joined the choir at the invitation of a close friend. I arrived at the church gate with a few minutes to spare, and having a good imagination, felt somewhat daunted at the prospect of following the church path through the ancient graveyard on my own. I was so pleased to settle into the circle of light illuminating the choir stalls in the dark church. We were preparing to sing carols on Christmas Day, less than a week away. It was quite a long rehearsal and I was pleased when the choirmaster said that it was over. But then he announced that we also needed to rehearse an anthem for the Fourth Sunday in Advent, which was the last Sunday before Christmas. The words of the anthem were taken from the epistle for the day, 'Rejoice in the Lord always; again I will say, Rejoice' (Philippians 4.4).

We practised the anthem again and again until the choirmaster felt we had mastered it. At one point he came across to me and put his face very close to mine – which was terrifying enough – before saying in a loud voice, 'Rejoice, boy! Let me see you smile when you sing this. Show that you are glad that the Lord is with you!' In my fear I found it hard to smile and look at the music and sing at the same time, but the words of that anthem became the first section of Scripture I truly learnt. Committed to memory, it entered my heart and took shape in my mind. Singing over and over 'Rejoice in the Lord', 'the Lord is at hand' and 'be anxious of nothing' in worship helped me know the reality of these words deep in my being, and enabled me not only to acknowledge and rejoice in a presence, but to smile because of it. Perhaps this is what Psalm 43 in the Book of Common Prayer means when it says: 'O put your trust in God: for I will yet give him thanks, which is the help of my countenance and my God.' Can trust in God affect not only the way you look at the world but also your actual appearance? Sometimes a good simple exercise is to follow the advice of my choirmaster: 'Smile, the Lord is with you.'

After the rehearsal, I couldn't sleep for thinking about the words of the anthem as they echoed through my mind,

'Rejoice for the Lord is at hand'. The choirmaster had also explained how Emmanuel meant that God is with us, and later in life I would realize that Advent is about being more alert and awake to the one who comes. It offers us an invitation to know that God is with us at every moment, and that he actively seeks us out. I have also tried to put into practice what the choirmaster said about smiling because God is with me!

One of my favourite saints as I grew older was St Francis, who often emphasized opening our lives to the joy of the Lord's presence. He found great delight in the poverty he adopted, showing that true joy comes from God and not from possessions. Indeed, a true indication of the Lord's presence in our lives is the joy we experience and express, for our God is a life-extending God. A faith that makes life feel diminished is not the true Christian faith. When the women who went to Jesus's tomb were told of the risen Lord, Matthew says, 'they left the tomb quickly with fear and great joy' (Matthew 28.8). When the risen Lord appeared to the disciples, John says, 'Then the disciples rejoiced when they saw the Lord' (John 20.20). Whenever God is truly known in a life, an awareness of joy will exist alongside. Nehemiah said, to encourage the people, 'the joy of the LORD is your strength' (Nehemiah 8.10). Our witness must be shown in our joy. How I like the prayer attributed to St Teresa of Avila: 'God deliver us from sour-faced saints.'

Still later, I would discover how Paul's entire letter to the Philippians is full of joy. Paul was used to the idea of rejoicing in God from his regular reading of the Psalms. For example:

> In your presence there is fullness of joy.
> (Psalm 16.11)

> My soul shall rejoice in the Lord.
> (Psalm 35.9)

And he is familiar with the concept of dwelling in God found in Psalms such as 139, which describes how God is all around us, encompassing us. When Paul goes to Athens and stands in front of the Areopagus, he tells the men of the city that God 'is not far from each one of us'. Then he quotes from an Athenian poem that says, 'In him we live and move and have our being' (see Acts 17.27–28).

You may not be surprised at Paul rejoicing in the Lord, though if you consider his situation at times, it should at least make you wonder! The letter to the Philippians was composed while he was being held under close house arrest in Rome, with a death sentence hanging over him. Paul has earlier been asked to leave the city of Philippi by the magistrates (Acts 16), after undergoing a severe flogging and an illegal imprisonment. Such persecution is still being suffered by the Church there, and he urges the Philippians not to fear what their opponents are putting them through, for he himself has gone through this and is still enduring it (Philippians 1.27–30). Indeed, it appears that Paul's reward for being faithful to his calling has been a life of many troubles (see his own account of these in 2 Corinthians 11.23–28). But the truth is that none of these early Christians are having an easy time, either, and they may well be feeling like returning to their old faith. It is this situation Paul is addressing as he writes to the Philippians in what is often called 'The Letter of Joy', for again and again the words 'joy' and 'rejoice' occur.

Paul is linked to his friends in Philippi by the joy of God's presence in prayer (Philippians 1.4); there is joy that Christ is proclaimed (1.18); the joy of the Philippians' faith in God (1.25); joy in their unity and fellowship in the Gospel (2.2); joy in the giving of one's life for Christ (2.17–18); joy in meeting and accepting another (2.25–30); the ability to rejoice in the Lord (3.1); and finally, the joy of standing firm in the Lord (4.1).

This celebration reaches its peak with the very words I learnt by heart in the choir: 'Rejoice in the Lord always; again I will say, Rejoice. Let your gentleness be known to everyone. The Lord is near' (4.4). Non-believers might find this pretty absurd advice to people facing a great deal of trouble! No doubt Paul had in mind Jesus's words: 'You have pain now; but I will see you again, and your heart will rejoice, and no one will take your joy from you.' There is something about Christian joy that is quite indestructible. Happiness depends on 'hap', that is on chance: joy is a gift and comes from the Lord. We are God's and nothing can separate us from his love in Christ Jesus. Because of this love, we are not perishable goods (John 3.16). Rejoice! One of the greatest ways to witness to our faith is to reveal the joy it brings – the joy of being loved, of being saved, and of having our very being in God, aware that God is in us. We need to explore this for ourselves every day.

Dietrich Bonhoeffer was imprisoned by the Nazis on 5 April 1943 (and would be executed two years later). Yet even in such circumstances, he could write of modern plays and literature:

On the whole, all the newest productions seem to me to be lacking in *hilaritas* – 'cheerfulness' – which is to be found in any really great and free intellectual achievement. One has always the impression of a some-what tortured and strained manufacture instead of creative activity in the open air.[2]

In another letter he would repeat the need for joy:

Now that's enough for today. When shall we be able to talk together again? Keep well, enjoy the beautiful country, spread *hilaritas* around you, and keep it in yourself too![3]

Reading Bonhoeffer should make us think more about what we are doing when we worship. Perhaps our devotions some-times appear as 'a somewhat tortured and strained manufacture instead of creative activity', when they should actually express our joy and love for God. I still worry when I hear a priest say 'Lift up your hearts', as if this is something pretty hard to do. And even when a priest does manage to sound joyful, there is often a dull, mumbling response of 'We lift them to the Lord' from the depths of the congregation, appearing to come from the soles of their feet rather than from their hearts. In the Holy Communion service, I like to be called the 'celebrant' (rather than the 'president', which has con-notations of power and control), as I believe my role is to lead the people into the joy of the Lord's presence.

Joy is meant to flow into all that we do, but it is a gift from God and we cannot create it ourselves. So many 'party people' spend their lives seeking joy, but it eludes them. I do not deny they may often find pleasure, but pleasure usually has a short shelf life, as the poet Robert Burns expresses beautifully in his poem *Tam o'Shanter*:

> But pleasures are like poppies spread,
> You seize the flower, its bloom is shed;
> Or like the snow falls in the river,
> A moment white – then melts for ever;
> Or like the borealis race,
> That flit ere you can point their place;
> Or like the rainbow's lovely form
> Evanishing amid the storm.

However, although Christians will experience joy, there will inevitably be days with some very cheerless things in them, and there is no point in displaying a false sense of euphoria in face of reality. When we are down, we can at least find comfort in the assurance of God's presence and love. I find the whole of Romans 8 powerful, but in particular these words:

> Who will separate us from the love of Christ? Will hardship, or distress, or persecution, or famine, or nakedness, or peril, or sword? As it is written, 'For your sake we are being killed all day long; we are accounted as sheep to be slaughtered.' No, in all these things we are more than conquerors through him who loved us. For I am convinced that neither death, nor life, nor angels, nor rulers, nor things present, nor things to come, nor powers, nor height, nor depth, nor anything else in all creation, will be able to separate us from the love of God in Christ Jesus our Lord.   (Romans 8.35–39)

Paul never denies the reality of what he is undergoing, but he does not let it overcome him because he is loved by God and cannot be separated from God or his love. He rejoices because he is in the Lord. Those of us who frequently feel rather less spiritually strong may find comfort, as I do, in a prayer from the Outer Hebrides. It expresses well the situation where we believe in the presence but are faced with clouds and darkness. This darkness is a reality, yet so is the presence of our God, and even when we do not feel the presence, we can still affirm it. I use this prayer often on cold dark days, when so much of the world seems in turmoil. You may like to learn it!

> Though the dawn breaks cheerless on this isle today,
> my spirit walks in a path of light.
> For I know my greatness.
> Thou hast built me a throne within Thy heart.
> I dwell safely within the circle of Thy care.
> I cannot for a moment fall out of the everlasting arms.
> I am on my way to glory.[4]

Even on the gloomiest days, we cannot fall out of the everlasting arms. Rejoice!

Exercises

1 Think upon these words

'In him we live and move and have our being.'

2 The 5p exercise

Pause Be still. Relax, let go of all troubled thoughts. Check your body and see that you are comfortable and have no areas of tension. Starting from your head, eyes, jaw and neck, move down and relax each part as much as possible. You need not do anything to be in God's presence, for he is with you. It is your own tension and busyness that prevents you from knowing him.

Presence Nothing you can do can make God more present than he is. Relax in his presence. There is no need to say anything, just enjoy being with God. If your mind wanders bring it back by saying to God, 'God you are here with me. I give my love to you.' Know that when God is with you, so are all his gifts. God brings his peace, his love, his forgiveness, his joy to you. All of this is for free, it cannot be earned; it is gratis, from God's grace. Seek God, not his gifts, and you will find what you need comes with him. Now, rejoice in God's presence and love.

Picture Read Philippians 4.4–7. Paul is under close house arrest and writing this letter to Christians who are in danger. What could he write? He could avoid facing difficult issues but he does not. Instead he writes, 'Rejoice in the Lord always; again I will say, Rejoice.' Can you think of a suggestion bolder than this? No doubt Paul had in mind the words of Jesus: 'You have pain now; but I will see you again, and your heart will rejoice, and no one will take your joy from you.' Paul then suggests to his readers, 'Let your gentleness be known to everyone.' The word for gentleness is *epieikeia* and describes a certain attitude towards people, 'something better than justice'. The strict laying down of the law can be severe because of its generality, but we are asked to treat each individual with respect and mercy and not to hamper their freedom – in the same way that God treats us. There is always the temptation to strike back with force when we feel hurt. Rather show you are one with God by revealing something of his characteristics. Be known for your mercy, forgiveness and kindness, your acceptance of people. It is undeniable that if our relationships with each other are wrong, they will affect our relationship with God. How do you picture the Christians in Philippi reacting to this piece of Paul's advice?

He adds a reminder, 'The Lord is near.' In our lives, in our sorrows as well as in our joys, the Lord is here. One of the worst things about any suffering is that it appears to separate us from others. Paul reminds us that the Lord is always with us. He is our strength and our support and it is wonderful to know that we are not alone. Rejoice! Rejoice, knowing that God is with you. It is very easy to doubt this but can you see it as a reality? Do you think the Philippians saw it this way?

Paul does not deny that he and his readers are living through troubled times. He writes, 'Do not worry about anything, but in everything by prayer and supplication with thanksgiving let your requests be made known to God.' Paul suggests we talk to God regularly. We should know him as our constant friend and helper and bring to him our hopes and fears, our sorrows and our joys. It is foolish to struggle as if we are alone, for we are not: God is with us. Trust in him knowing he cares for you. Rejoice!

Paul then expresses what the outcome of this faithfulness is: 'And the peace of God, which surpasses all understanding, will guard your hearts and your minds in Christ Jesus' (4.7). It is when we know we are not toiling alone, that we are not forsaken or forgotten and will not be overcome, that a new peace enters our lives. This peace is the free gift of God's presence. Again we embrace the underlying theme that God made us, God cares for us, God loves us, and God is with us. If we allow ourselves to rest in his presence we will begin to know his peace. Peace, like joy, is a gift from God. We need to learn to accept it and live it. Rejoice!

Picture the assurance of Paul in prison. He is ready to face death, knowing this cannot separate him from God and the fullness of eternal life.

Ponder Go through each of the above paragraphs and think how they relate to the way you live.

How often do you rejoice that you are in the Lord and that he is in you?

Do you see that all relationships are related? If you fall out with someone, you cause a break in your full relationship to God. How do you rate this statement?

Does your life reflect that the Lord is near?

Can you improve your relationship with God by talking to him and bringing to him the realities of your life?

Do you let his presence and his peace flow into your life?

Promise to improve your own relationships with others and with God.

3 Pray

A prayer that looks to the source of our joy and affirms our trust in God:

> Even though the day be laden and my task is dreary, and my strength is small, a song keeps singing in my heart. For I know that I am Thine. I am part of Thee. Thou art kin to me and all times are in Thy hand.[5]

10

❧ *Journeying on in God* ❧

I arise today
Through a mighty strength,
the invocation of the Trinity,
Through belief in the threeness,
Through confession of the oneness
Of the Creator of Creation.

I arise today
Through the strength of Christ's birth with His
   baptism,
Through the strength of His crucifixion with His
   burial,
Through the strength of His resurrection with His
   ascension,
Through the strength of His descent for the
   judgement of Doom.[1]

The meeting between the disciples and the risen Lord on the mountain is in many senses beyond description. Drawing us into 'the cloud of unknowing', the Ascension is an event we cannot fully understand, and we may as well stop trying to find clear and comforting explanations of it! Let's accept instead that we are facing a mystery. We are before 'the presence that disturbs' – and yet that presence surrounds us in love. You may like to read Matthew's account in 28.16–20,

119

which is the fulfilment of the risen Lord's promise in verse 10 to Mary Magdalene and the other Mary: 'Do not be afraid; go and tell my brothers to go to Galilee; there they will see me.' The women are not simply to stay where Jesus is but 'to go' and tell the disciples. It is for this reason that Mary Magdalene has been called the apostle of the apostles. She, who loved him deeply, is the first to see the risen Lord and the first to be sent by him.

Mary delivers her message and the 11 go to Galilee. It is worth noting they are one down: Judas has chosen his own way which has led to darkness and his death. The others return to their homes, to their roots, to where the ministry of Jesus began. Their subsequent meeting with the risen Lord on the seashore (John 21.1–25) may be in preparation for the next step – the Ascension, which takes place on an unnamed mountain (Matthew 28.16). In Matthew, as in much of the Old Testament, the mountain is a symbol of the presence, the power and the authority of God: high and holy, mountains may put us in mind of what are often described as 'thin places'. (See Matthew 4.8; 5.1; 14.23; 15.29; 17.1 for other occasions on which Jesus went up high mountains.)

When the disciples saw the Lord, they worshipped him; but some doubted (see Matthew 28.17). The men in this little group are far from perfect human beings, and none is remembered as a visionary. There seems to be no feeling of absolute certainty about what they are seeing, but then, there never is with faith. John may be implying in the phrase 'but some doubted' that Thomas, who has earlier doubted the disciples' story of the resurrection, is present (see John 20.26–29). There is only one other time when this word for doubt, *distazo*, is used in the New Testament, and that is when Peter seeks to walk on the water, takes his eyes off Jesus and then doubts (Matthew 14.31). *Distazo* carries the meaning of not being certain of what is happening. Jesus calls disciples who are not 100 per cent sure into the unknown. The disciples are unclear about what they are called to, or even who is doing the calling, but they do put their faith in Jesus. They have a real, living, trusting relationship with him. Later, to bring their number back up to 12, they choose Matthias who, like them, has known Jesus personally from the beginning and has been a witness to his resurrection (Acts 1.21–26).

The risen Lord, who has appeared in the garden, in a room in Jerusalem, on the road to Emmaus and by the seashore in Galilee, now appears on a mountain and seeks to encourage the disciples, saying, 'All authority in heaven and earth has been given to me.' Jesus assures them of his power. He is the one who was crucified, dead and buried: the one who has triumphed over death. In the beginning of creation, there was no division between heaven and earth – all was unity. But by chapter 4 of Genesis, the self-will and disobedience of human beings has created a fracture in the universe. In the Lord's Prayer we pray for this fracture to be healed: 'Thy kingdom come on earth as it is in heaven'. Matthew's Gospel concludes by revealing the end of a broken world through the vision of Emmanuel, God among us. In the symbolism of the Temple veil torn in two (Matthew 27.1), heaven and earth are again one, and there is no division into sacred and secular, for all is holy. This has been made possible through Christ's obedience to the will of the Father. God's will is done and the kingdom of heaven is at hand.

After telling the disciples of his authority over heaven and earth, Jesus gives them a purpose: 'Go therefore and make disciples of all nations, baptizing them in the name of the Father and of the Son and of the Holy Spirit, and teaching them to obey everything that I have commanded you' (Matthew 28.19–20). What a task for 11 ordinary souls! There is to be no staying cosily on the mountain or in Galilee. They are instructed to 'Go out into *all* the world'. How overwhelmed must they feel? Where will they start? What will be asked of them? What will they say? Like their father in the faith, Abraham, they are being sent into the unknown. They are not scholars, theologians, orators, nor even particularly confident, but they will go. Why? Because they have the greatest credential of all: the Lord is with them and they will not be on their own, for 'remember, I am with you always, to the end of the age' (Matthew 28.20). 'Always' has the meaning of every day. Jesus is here, in his risen power, strengthening and guiding us, each day of our lives. The communicating of his presence is the very strength and purpose of the disciples' work.

The longer ending of Mark's Gospel says, 'And they went out and proclaimed the good news everywhere, while the Lord worked with them and confirmed the message by the signs that accompanied it' (Mark 16.20). There is something about people who walk with God that speaks louder than their words. Bede says of St Aidan of Lindisfarne and his followers:

> . . . they lived as they taught. He never sought or cared for worldly possession, and he loved to give away to the poor who chanced to meet him whatever he received

from kings or wealthy folk. Whether in town or country, he always travelled on foot unless compelled to ride: and whatever people he met on his walks, he stopped and spoke to them. If they were heathen he urged them to be baptized; and if they were Christian, he strengthened their faith, and inspired them by word and deed to live a good life and to be generous to others.[2]

Aidan's style was very much that of the early disciples, and this man who walked with God helped to convert England.

Baptism is not a magic act, but an outward and visible sign of a spiritual reality. It tells us we are *all* immersed in the very being of God. Medieval thinkers stated that only Christians are baptized, only Christians are the possessors of divine blessing. But the truth is that we are all in God's love, in God's power, in God's hand, and God is in every one of us. This is an awesome mystery which, once we begin to explore it, transfigures our lives and our approach to others. To be baptized means to be thoroughly immersed in something, in the way that a fish is immersed in the sea. This is why these words of the poet Kabir are inscribed on a fountain in India:

I laugh when I hear the fish in the water are thirsty.
I laugh when I hear that man goes in search of God.

Pause and appreciate what God has given you: the gift of his presence. 'Do you not know that you are God's temple and God's Spirit dwells in you? If anyone destroys God's temple, God will destroy that person. For God's temple is holy, and you are that temple' (1 Corinthians 3.16–17). Let's consider the implications of this. Once a year the high priest – and only the high priest – was permitted to enter into the holy of holies where God's presence dwelt. Now, after the crucifixion and resurrection of Jesus, the veil that had hidden God's presence has been torn in two, and the result of this is that God is to be found in every living person: even in you! Obviously, all of us need to take care when dealing with his other dwelling places – the people we meet. It is our task to open the eyes of those who are blind to the love and presence of God.

Doing things in the 'name of God' does not mean taking on his name as we know it. Rather it means being one with him and knowing he is one with us: God's name is the very being of God. To take his name in vain is less to do with swearing than with misusing his power and distorting his love.

After what they have experienced, the disciples are aware that their God is a living reality who is with them always. This is the Good News! God is among us. He is not an exclusive property who belongs to one set of people, or to religious people only. He is the God of all people, and dwells in each one of us. This is what the disciples have been sent out to proclaim. They have not been sent to *take* God anywhere, but to help people to discover that *God is with them*. How different to some Christian missions which set out believing they were possessors of God – a god kept in a book and caged up in church and sacraments, selective about whom he loved. Such missions were triumphal in their approach and often destroyed the culture, wisdom and insight of those they turned into 'European Christians'. In this way we lost so much of value in our world. Those who believe they are the sole possessors of Christ still frighten me today. Instead of going out with such an attitude, our impulse should be to meet God in the other. Our privilege as the catholic (in the universal sense) Church is to believe that God is with 'all people, at all times and in all places' and to help others discover that they are loved by God and that they dwell in him.

Consider this: how different might it be if making disciples of all nations did not mean converting non-believers to Christianity, as has come to be understood in our churches, but helping them to discover God within them and about them? Enabling them to see that through God's love revealed in Christ Jesus, life is eternal? We can show this by our own style of living and through the way we deal with others. You cannot deliberately harm another human who has God dwelling in him: this awesome mystery – evident to others in our lives however unworthy we might feel – should inspire reverence.

Jesus also commands us to heal the sick, bring justice to the oppressed, house the homeless and relieve the poor in all the world: to show that the good news reveals a better way to live together, a better way to deal with each other, a better way to nurture life and to love and to do justice than we have managed before. We will then be fulfilling the teaching of Jesus, which appears only three chapters earlier than the Ascension story:

> Then the king will say to those at his right hand, 'Come, you that are blessed by my father, inherit the kingdom prepared for you from the foundation of the world; for I was hungry and you gave me food, I was thirsty and you gave me something to drink. I was a stranger and you welcomed me, I was naked and you gave me clothing,

I was sick and you took care of me, I was in prison and you visited me.' Then the righteous will answer him: 'Lord, when was it that we saw you hungry and gave you food, or thirsty and gave you something to drink? . . . And when was it that we saw you sick or in prison and visited you?' And the king will answer them, 'Truly, I tell you, just as you did it to one of the least of these who are members of my family, you did it to me.'

(Matthew 25.34–40)

The only way to unity and justice, the only way to true freedom is to see that we are one in God and that God is in each of us. This does not mark the end of the awesome journey, but a new beginning. Learning to walk with God and reveal that he is in us is the way of contemplation and the way of action. It will not always be a simple journey. We will often have to travel in faith, for we do not possess all the answers. But we do have a God who is with us. Continue living in his presence, in his peace, in his power: journey on in the name of God, Father, Son and Holy Spirit.

Exercises

1 Think upon these words

Reflect on these words of St Augustine of Hippo and take them to heart:

I was slow to love you, Lord,
your age-old beauty is still as new to me:
I was slow to love you!
You were within me,
yet I stayed outside

seeking you there;
in my ugliness I grabbed at
the beautiful things of your creation.
Already you were with me,
but I was still far from you.
The things of this world kept me away: I did not
   know then
that if they had not existed through you
they would not have existed at all.
Then you called me
and your cry overcame my deafness;
you shone out
and your light overcame my blindness;
you surrounded me with your fragrance
and I breathed it in,
so that now I yearn for more of you;
I tasted you
and now I am hungry and thirsty for you;
you touched me,
and now I burn with longing for your peace.[3]

Are you still looking outside for God who is with you and within you?

2 The 5p exercise

Pause Check your body. Is it comfortable and relaxed? Let go of all tension in your hands, feet and neck, and be still and at ease. Try to keep your mind empty, but if thoughts invade, concentrate on your breathing. Say quietly, 'Lord God,' and repeat this with each breath. Breathe deeply . . . slowly . . . comfortably: You may like to say 'Lord' as you inhale

127

and 'God' as you exhale. Then be quiet and still. This is your journey into awareness of God. Be open to knowing him; to realizing God is with you and within you. This should always be an awesome time.

Presence God is with you: you live and move in him. This is the reason for creating space – not for knowledge, not for peace, not even for love, but for God himself who comes to you. (No doubt you will then receive his gifts also.) Open yourself to God's presence. Seek to be aware of the great mystery of God that is about you. He will not force himself upon you; you need be open to him, to welcome him. You cannot imagine his presence or create it yourself; only open your life to him. Try and relax in the presence as you would in the sun on a nice day. After a time of stillness, you can affirm quietly: 'You Lord are . . . You Lord are with me . . . Lord, I am with you . . . You Lord are here . . . Lord.'

Picture Read Matthew 28.16–20. There are many illustrations of the Ascension, but few capture the mystery of the occasion. First, see the event as related by Matthew, then consider how you would paint it or show it on film so it did not look too odd. It is always hard to capture mystery in words or art. Matthew avoids any mention of the actual Ascension because he does not want to imply Jesus is leaving us. There is no mention of a cloud, depicting the hidden presence, because God is within us. Try and capture the disciples' reaction to being told to go and make disciples, baptizing them in the name of the Father and of the Son and of the Holy Spirit, and teaching them to obey everything Jesus has commanded them. Try and capture the disciples' reaction to the enormity of their task; then try to imagine the assurance they would feel knowing the presence of Jesus was with them always.

Ponder Like Abraham the disciples are told to 'go' without much more direction. Like Jacob they discover the Lord is in this place. Like Moses they are promised his presence. Like Elijah they hear the voice of the Lord. Like Isaiah they discover the Lord is in control and heaven and earth are full of his glory.

Are you still hiding from God like Adam?

Have you come home to the Father, as a prodigal returning, or are you still refusing to come in?

Have you learnt to rejoice in the presence: to see Christ in others and to be Christ to others?

Do you treat yourself with respect as 'the temple of God', and others the same?

This is not the end of the awesome journey; travel on in him and know he is with you and in you.

Promise to recall that God is with you throughout the day. At set intervals, remember 'The Lord is here.' In times of stress, temptation or weakness it is good to affirm, 'The Lord is here.' When you meet someone, know the Lord is in them, though sometimes very hidden.

3 Pray

I arise today in the presence of the Father,
In the peace of the Saviour,
In the power of the Spirit,
In the Three and in the One.

I arise today in the love of God,
In the forgiveness of God,
In the grace of God,
Given to me and to all people.

I arise today to see God in my life:
To meet God in others,
To see him in their lives,
In his love and in his glory.

I arise today journeying in God,
To open the eyes that are blind,
To warm the hearts that are cold,
To bring us all home to God:
That we all may rejoice in him.

⚡ *Notes* ⚡

Introduction
1 Pierre Teilhard de Chardin, *Le Milieu divin* (London: Fontana, 1964), p. 112.

1 Where are you?
1 William Wordsworth, *Intimations of Immortality*, st. 4 (London: Oxford University Press, 1926), pp. 462–3.
2 GREAT IS THY FAITHFULNESS by Thomas O. Chisholm. © 1923, Ren. 1951 Hope Publishing Company, Carol Stream, IL 60188. All rights reserved. Used by permission.
3 D. H. Lawrence, 'The Egotist', *The Complete Poems of D. H. Lawrence* (Ware: Wordsworth Editions, 2002), p. 497.
4 Alexander Carmichael, *Carmina Gadelica*, Vol. 1 (Edinburgh: Scottish Academic Press, 1983), p. 69.

2 A divine discontent
1 Ancient hymn, author unknown, attributed to St Columba.
2 William Wordsworth, *Lines composed above Tintern Abbey*, lines 94–102.
3 G. R. D. McLean, *Poems of the Western Highlanders* (London: SPCK, 1961), p. 55.
4 Nora Chadwick, *Age of the Saints in the Early Celtic Church* (London: Oxford University Press, 1961), p. 64.
5 *Gerard Manley Hopkins: Poems and Prose*, selected and edited by W. H. Gardner (London: Penguin, 1974), p. 27.
6 Attributed to Sir Francis Drake.

3 The other in our midst

1 Celtic Rune by Kenneth MacLeod.
2 Thomas Ogletree, *Hospitality to the Stranger* (Philadelphia: Fortress Press, 1985), pp. 2–3.
3 Pierre Teilhard de Chardin, *Le Milieu divin* (London: Fontana, 1964), p. 145 (adapted).

4 Liminal places

1 From 'The Kingdom of God', by Francis Thompson (1913), *Selected Poems* (London: Methuen/Burns and Oates, no date), p. 133.
2 Antoine de Saint-Exupéry, *The Little Prince* (London: Penguin, 1962), pp. 91–2.
3 *Gerard Manley Hopkins: Poems and Prose*, selected and edited by W. H. Gardner (London: Penguin, 1974), p. 120.
4 Christopher Devlin SJ (ed.), *The Sermons and Devotional Writings of Gerard Manley Hopkins* (London: Oxford University Press, 1959), p. 195.
5 Pierre Teilhard de Chardin, *Le Milieu divin* (London: Fontana, 1964), p. 112.
6 Jean-Pierre de Caussade, *The Sacrament of the Present Moment*, tr. Kitty Muggeridge (London: Fount, 1981), p. 34.
7 David Adam, *Tides and Seasons* (London: SPCK, 1989), p. 7.

5 Hearts on fire

1 R. S. Thomas, *Collected Poems, 1945–1990* (London: Phoenix Giant, an imprint of Orion Books Ltd, © R. S. Thomas 1993), p. 302. Reproduced by permission of The Orion Publishing Group, London.
2 Elizabeth Barrett Browning, *Aurora Leigh* (1857), bk 7, lines 821–6.
3 Pierre Teilhard de Chardin, *Le Milieu divin* (London: Fontana, 1964), p. 64.

6 Strength in our weakness

1 From 'No worst, there is none', by Gerard Manley Hopkins, *Gerard Manley Hopkins: Poems and Prose*, selected and edited by W. H. Gardner (London: Penguin, 1974), p. 61.

2 Alec King, *Wordsworth and the Artist's Vision* (London: Athlone Press, 1966), pp. 20–4.
3 C. S. Lewis, *The Lion, the Witch and the Wardrobe* (London: Harper-Collins Children's Books, 2001), p. 203.
4 Alexander Carmichael (ed.), *Carmina Gadelica*, Vol. 3 (Edinburgh: Scottish Academic Press, 1976), p. 51.
5 David Adam, *The Edge of Glory* (London: SPCK/Triangle, 1985), p. 7.

7 The shaking of the foundations

1 From 'The Kingdom of God', by Francis Thompson (1913), *Selected Poems* (London: Methuen/Burns and Oates, no date), p. 132.
2 David Adam, *Walking the Edges* (London: SPCK, 2003), pp. 69–70.
3 H. F. Lyte (1793–1847).
4 Pierre Teilhard de Chardin, *Le Milieu divin* (London: Fontana, 1975), p. 66.

8 Coming home

1 St Augustine Soliloquies 1.3a, Murray Watts, *Praying with St Augustine* (London: SPCK, 1987), pp. 87–8.
2 *Selections from Ancient Irish Poetry*, tr. Kuno Meyer (London: Constable, 1928), p. 25.
3 John Keble (1792–1866).
4 H. A. Williams, *True Resurrection* (London: Mitchell Beazley, 1972), p. 33.
5 Julian of Norwich (1342–*c*.1416), quoted in *The SPCK Book of Christian Prayer* (London: SPCK, 1995).

9 Rejoicing in the Lord

1 St Patrick.
2 *Bonhoeffer's Letters and Papers from Prison* (London: SCM Press, 1971), p. 189.
3 *Bonhoeffer's Letters*, p. 232.
4 Alistair Maclean, *Hebridean Altars* (Edinburgh: Grant and Murray, 1937), p. 55.
5 Maclean, *Hebridean Altars*, p. 60.

10 Journeying on in God

1 'The Deer's Cry', tr. Kuno Meyer, which is credited to St Patrick.

2 Bede, *A History of the English Church and People*, Book III, Chapter 5, tr. Leo Sherley-Price (London: Penguin, 1979).

3 St Augustine, Confessions 10.27, Murray Watts, *Praying with Saint Augustine*, (London: SPCK, 1987), p. 19.